What Fish *See*: Understanding optics and color shifts for designing lures and flies

Colin J. Kageyama, O.D., F.C.O.V.D.

Illustrations by Vic Erickson

A *Frank* mato

PORTLAND

Thank you

To Paul Johnson, Ron Kovac, Jed Davis, and Bill Herzog—four men I have never met but whose books I have read and enjoyed for years.

To Nick Amato, Bill Williamson, and Mike Laverty for their support and input.

To Bruce Harpole and the Oregon Fishing Club for giving me the opportunity to learn about fishing for steelhead and salmon and meet many great fishermen, including Joe Madrid . . . a great fisherman and an even better friend.

To "B.G." at G.I. Joe's for being the first stores to carry the Steelhead Color Selector, and to Mepps/Sheldon's for being the first lure company to use this information in lure design.

To my wife Valerie for staying with me through thick and thin and for trying to understand why someone would rush off at 4:30 in the morning, then practice catch-and-release and not even bring something home for dinner! It is not easy being married to a fisherman.

All inquiries should be addressed to:
Frank Amato Publications, Inc.
P.O. Box 82112, Portland, Oregon 97282
503•653•8108

Photographs by Colin J. Kageyama • Illustrations by Vic Erickson
Cover photo by Jim Schollmeyer
Book and Cover Design: Kathy Johnson

Printed in Canada
Softbound ISBN: 1-57188-140-9
3 5 7 9 10 8 6 4 2

Section I: Personal Search

Section II: Scientists At Work

Looking Down
Water Conditions

Section III: Fishermen Trying To Use The Science

Section IV: Using The Science Of Underwater Visibility

Section VII: The Conclusion

Steelhead Fishing Is About Problem Solving
Why Do Fishermen Know So Little About What Fish See?
Don't Trust What It Looks Like On The Shelf!
KISS: Keep It Short And Simple
Final Note

Section I
Personal Search

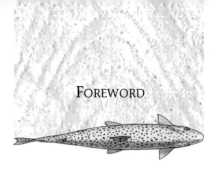

FOREWORD

"The Most Innovative Approach To Fishing That I Have Ever Heard!"

THAT'S WHAT NICK AMATO SAID WHEN I FIRST TALKED TO HIM IN January of 1996. Over the past three years, I have caught steelhead at a rate that some anglers consider unbelievable. In this book, I have described the methods and the theories that I developed. Steelhead fishing was my inspiration for writing this book, but this material has important applications to many other types of fishing. I believe that this may be one of the most important books written about fishing in recent years. The information in *What Fish See* has the power to transform the fishing tackle industry.

This book attempts to explain why certain colored lures are more effective in certain water conditions. Other attempts at using science to explain fish behavior have failed either because the researcher was not a fisherman or the because the writer did not have an advanced understanding of optics, physiology, and color. Many fine outdoor writers have reached inaccurate conclusions on the link between science and fishing because they did not understand the flaws in the experimental research being performed.

This book could actually be split into areas:
- How I discovered the link between color and fishing
- How colors change under water
- How fishermen can use this science
- Quality control and fishing lure colors

The Challenge...

It was a challenge to make this topic simple enough to be of value to the average fisherman. Much of the research was done by scientists who had no interest in fishing. Reading these scientific journals required hundreds of hours of study. Five factors make me uniquely qualified to discuss this research and its applications to fishing:

- •I have post-graduate level training in optics, neurophysiology, color, and vision perception. I have seen fishing articles written by doctors, fisheries biologists, and other college-educated professionals. What these people lacked was the background in optics and vision perception.
- •I have spent many hours under water observing fishing lures. There is no substitute for actually going under water and looking at how different fishing lures appear. Most authors who write about fishing lure colors never inspected their fishing lures underwater to test their theories.
- •My success rate places me in the top 1% of steelheaders in the Pacific Northwest. I can catch ten to fifteen steelhead a month. I have a good idea of what works under different conditions. I have caught steelhead under a variety of conditions, with all the major types of lures.
- •I am a professional lure designer for one of the world's best-known fishing lure companies. I have experience in how a major lure company designs and tests their fishing lures.
- •I am an inventor with patents pending for the first underwater simulation system to determine the most effective fishing lure color combinations for a given water condition. I understand the problems of educating the public about new ideas and concepts.

How To Study This Book...

This is probably going to be the most technical fishing book that you have ever read. For this reason, I suggest that you study this book in steps. Don't try to read it cover to cover on your first try. If you do so, it is likely that you will get confused. On the other hand, once you get it, I think you'll be surprised at how much sense it makes and how simple it all seems.

I suggest you study the book in the following manner. Read the Introduction, chapters 4, 10, 12, 22, and then carefully study the pictures on pages 129-152. The photographs are the most important things that you need to understand in this book. Pay particular attention to how the underwater backgrounds appear to change as you look down, straight, or up. One of the pictures demonstrates how light-colored fish seem to blend in with the sand and sky, but give high contrast against dark rocks. These pictures show why fishing lure designers should take into account the changing underwater background. Working through these six sections will give you a good overview.

The next step is to go over every diagram and try to understand them. Once you do these first two steps, then try to read the entire book. Spend extra time trying to understand how the diagrams relate to fishing myths you have heard.

Taking It To The Next Level...

Bill Herzog wrote that questioning the accepted highest level of any technique is right because raising any steelhead technique to a new level of effectiveness is always a possibility. All great steelheaders seem to raise their skills to another level.

The information contained in this book is my attempt to raise steel heading to another level. This book questions many fishing myths that are widely accepted as truths. In the Pacific Northwest, many experts claim that it takes a beginner five years to learn how to catch steelhead. Less than 8% of all steelheaders catch over ten fish a year and fishing in recent years has been so poor than many have given up entirely. It took me slightly over two years to go from a beginner to a fisherman catching ten steelhead or salmon a month. I did this all from shore, without a boat, and within an hour's drive of the Portland Metro area.

In each of the past three years, I have always had at least one month where I caught ten summer steelhead and one month that I have caught at least ten winter steelhead. I have averaged well over ten steelhead or salmon a month in the last eighteen months that I have fished. In the last two-hundred days that I have fished, I have seen only ten steelhead landed. Seven of these ten steelhead were landed by people that I took fishing and four of these were ones that I hooked and passed on the pole. I have not fished areas that had a high catch rate. I do not attempt to catch large numbers of steelhead. I usually quit after catching two and always quit after catching three.

I do catch some salmon but I target them less than ten days a year. Most of my salmon were incidental catches when in pursuit of steelhead. I estimate that I have accidentally caught in excess of two-thousand trout in the past three years, while fishing for summer steelhead. Because of these accidents, I know these tactics work very well on salmon and trout, as well as steelhead. I think a big reason for my success is that I look at a fishing lure and its presentation from the standpoint of what it looks like under water.

What lures are easiest for the fish to see under water? How can fishermen use this information?

This book describes concepts that have never been explained to the fishing public, information that I feel is far too valuable to be kept a secret. I have met guides and fishing-store owners who claim that the colors of fishing lures are only affected in water over 100 feet deep. These experts are wrong! I will show you pictures of fishing lures that have changed color in water five feet deep!

A small group of fishing-store owners, guides, and tackle companies have told me that they hope this information never reaches the public. An executive from one company has said that this information could make his inventory obsolete! Virtually hundreds of lures and fishing materials have been poorly designed and intended to catch fishermen and not fish.

I wonder how many millions of flies have been tied with materials that look bright in air and turn black under water! I wonder how many millions of spinners have been sold with shank tubing that turns black under water? How many hundreds of hours have you spent fishing these poorly designed products? Poor design, quality control, and fishing myths about what is actually happening underwater pose a problem that has affected millions of anglers.

As Bill Herzog has written, "Question the highest accepted level of steelhead technique, lure design, and expertise." Using special tools, underwater photography, and insights that modify my fishing technique. I hope to show you how fishing for steelhead and salmon can be taken to the next level.

I started this book with the intent of describing the applications of underwater optics to steelhead fishing. I have expanded it to include applications for freshwater species (such as walleye, musky, panfish, kokanee, trout), as well as saltwater fishing. I believe that this is a major breakthrough. Read this book and keep an open mind. The information presented here has forever changed the way I look at a river when I am fishing. Because of this information, I have learned *What Fish See.*

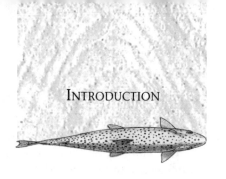

Seeing Through
The Eyes Of A Fish

IT'S A TOUGH LIFE FOR A YOUNG STEELHEAD FRY, ONE OF SEVERAL thousand eggs planted by its parents in a shallow gravel pit. Most of its brothers and sisters will be eaten by predators long before they are a year old. Its visual system allows it a wide field of view to look for potential dangers. It is well adapted to seeing the large amounts of red light reaching these shallow pools, with the visual pigment **porphryopsin** being the most common in its eyes. If someone could give it a color vision test, they would find an animal with peak sensitivity to red light.

After becoming a smolt, it has the genetic urge to go downstream until it reaches saltwater. Once in the ocean, chemical changes occur in its body that allow it to survive in saltwater. Its eyes change so that the dominant photochemical in its eyes become **rhodopsin**—similar to the visual pigment in human eyes used for night vision. In the dark depths of the sea, the light reaching the fry is largely blue and green. Thus it is well-served by having photochemicals in its eyes that are sensitive to blue and green light.

The fry is fortunate enough to survive the next few years, it will return to fresh water as a mature adult. Something in its genetic programming tells it to return to the bays, tidewater, and freshwater that it inhabited as a smolt. Slowly a number of physical changes occur in the fry's body to prepare it for the next stage in its life. Its eyes begin to change and become adapted to a brighter environment. The fry is now living under 2 to 5 feet of shallow water, compared to the deep ocean that had been home only a month ago.

The color-sensitive cells in its eyes begin to convert back to **porphryopsin** and its eyes regain their peak sensitivity to red light. The fry sees countless sticks, pebbles, rocks, shiny pieces of spinning metal and small pieces of brightly colored Styrofoam. Some of these it picks up, others it ignores. Why the fry does this, it does not know. It is a creature of instinct, since its brain is about the size of a pea, and its instincts tell it that it must continue to move upstream.

As the fry becomes a mature adult, it may develop some bright red markings. The increased red sensitivities of its eyes make it easier to find others in its species, as well as eggs deposited by large females. The fry's eyes also prepare it to be able to see in water so bright that it would have blinded the fry only a month earlier.

As it moves around in a deep pool, the fry drifts down into a tailout, and then back up to the head...just under the foaming "chop." Sometimes everything it sees is deep green, while other times it is in the middle of white bubbles. It sees the silver flash of other fish, some dark brown nymphs, green moss, and some leaves floating in the water. These are all familiar and the fry ignores them. Something catches its eye, something pink and white, with an interesting movement. The fry opens its mouth to feel it, to identify it, and feels the bite of something sharp in its mouth.

What Fish See is an attempt to describe to fishermen something that has never been described before—the underwater vision of a salmonid. This is a complex problem because the vision of steelhead and most anadromous fish changes as they go from salt- to freshwater. The vision of these fish is also dependent on underwater color shifts that take place as a function of water clarity. Their vision also depends on the direction that they are looking and the color of underwater backgrounds.

The underwater experience of fish is very different from the experience humans have viewing objects through air. Extensive scientific research has been done on these subjects, little of which has reached the fishing public. The steelhead is considered to be an extremely difficult fish to catch. Many people invest years without catching a single fish.

I am convinced that much of the difficulty that people have with catching "Mr. Steelhead" has to do with the type of conditions in which they pursue them. For most people, the steelhead is the only fish that they pursue in water that is both cloudy and moving. Lures move rapidly past this fish's holding area, which means that they must be presented accurately in spite of complex current interaction. Limited visibility means that there is little margin for error.

The two most important factors for success in river-fishing for steelhead (and salmon) are knowledge about location of fish and proper presentation. Understanding color and the fish's underwater vision serves to increase your margin of error. High-visibility colors may give the fish extra seconds to spot and react to a lure in moving water.

There are many myths and inaccurate statements that have been made concerning this subject. It is my hope that this book increases your enjoyment of this sport, as well as your catch rate.

15

History Of The Search

I remember fishing trips that I took as a child, forty years ago. Fishing has always been an important part of my life. When I went to college and became a doctor of optometry, I never considered the possibility that I might someday attempt to combine optics with fishing.

The steelhead is one of the most prized game fish in North America. I remember my father's good friend who took numerous trips to Oregon over a ten-year period and was never able to land one. I remember thinking, "How could catching a fish be that difficult?"

In September of '93 I had the opportunity to find out. I sold my practice and moved to Oregon. I did everything that a beginner should do—read the books, bought the equipment, selected a few prime rivers, and decided to learn them all very well. In the first year, I went fishing twelve times. I did not get a single bite.

In September '94, I joined the Oregon Fishing Club. This put me in touch with a number of fine anglers. In my second year, I went fishing 32 times and was rewarded with eight fish. I read an article in a local newspaper that said only 8% of Oregon steelheaders caught ten fish a year.

In June of 1995, I made my first discovery concerning the types of lures that are most visible underwater. I found extensive scientific research that described underwater color shifts, how fish see, and the light-bending properties of water that answered many questions I had about fishing. In August of '95, I met Joe Madrid, one of the top steelheaders in the state. Joe taught me some important lessons about how fish hold in different parts of a river.

Over the next seventeen months, I went steelhead/salmon fishing about twelve months. I skipped over five months from March until August 1996, because I was busy coaching my son's baseball team. During the remaining twelve months, I went steelhead/salmon fishing 83 times. I was able to catch 121 steelhead/salmon in rivers and streams. I caught at least one fish on 56 different days, a 67% success rate.

January of 1997 was my best month to date, when I landed sixteen winter steelhead in slightly over thirty hours of fishing. I realize that there are a few rivers in the Pacific Northwest where an expert could catch this many steelhead in a single day. These type of rivers are not for me.

I like to fish places where fishing is considered mediocre. The challenge is part of the fun. I would rather catch a single steelhead on a river where 90% of the anglers are getting skunked, than fish a river where catching a dozen fish might be considered routine. The techniques described in this book were developed in small rivers, where the total run was usually between 300 and 1300 steelhead.

As I look over the manuscript of this book, it is hard to believe that this

16

information was developed over a period of less than four years. People say that practice makes perfect and that the best fishing is learned through trial and error. I believe that learning how to fish can be a very inefficient process when you do not understand what you are actually trying. I believe that my rapid progress was made possible through my understanding of underwater optics and fish eyes.

In 1987, I purchased a book which was written by Paul Johnson, titled *The Scientific Angler*. This book contained many photographs of paints which appeared to change color in deep water. My real success in the art of steelhead fishing began in November of 1994, when I first began to understand the importance of these pictures.

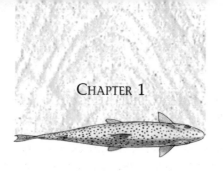

CHAPTER 1

History Of My Search

IN *THE SCIENTIFIC ANGLER,* PAUL JOHNSON PUBLISHED A SERIES OF pictures that showed what different types of paints looked like under water. He painted a board with seven patches of fluorescent paint and seven patches of bright non-fluorescent paint. As he took this board down 20 to 40 feet into clear blue sea water, eight colors began to blend into the pale blue of the water. Three colors appeared to turn black, while three others continued to glow brightly. At a distance, only one of these fourteen colors stayed bright and visible.

As I looked at these pictures I was interested but realized that the information was not very useful to me. Some colors turned black under water, while others stayed bright. But this picture gave me no information about the fishing lures I personally was using. I did not have a technique to gain this information. I looked at these pictures for several years without understanding their significance.

In November of 1994, a patient came to my office after being hit in the eye. I placed some fluorescent dyes in the eye and examined it with a medical optical filter. As I looked at the patient's eye, I noticed things that I had seen hundreds of times before. The filter made the blood look black, while the fluorescent dyes made parts of the eye glow brightly. But this time it was different! For some reason I began thinking about the underwater picture that I had seen in Paul Johnson's book. I wondered to myself, "Is this the same thing? Could the solution to my fishing problems be that simple?"

I took several sheets of bright-colored steelhead spinner tape and attempted to duplicate Paul Johnson's multi-colored plate. I went into a dark room and viewed the colors under my medical filter. I found that the effect matched a picture that Johnson described as a "deep-water color shift." Through trial and error I found that I could use the same filter differently to duplicate what Johnson described as a "long-distance underwater color shift."

I took some trips to fish ladders and observed that the color of fish appeared to change in muddy water. I found some articles in *Scientific American* that described the types of light transmission that took place in different water conditions. I began looking for filters that would match these types of light transmission. I developed a set of ten different optical filters which matched underwater light transmission of water types ranging from clear to muddy.

I found extensive research about fish eyes and fish vision never before discussed in a fishing magazine. Much of this information was extremely technical and even I had difficulty understanding some of the papers. I spent a lot of time looking up optical terms and concepts in some of my old text-books on vision and optics. The challenge was then to test the theory.

I began talking to fishing experts and guides. I found that I could predict which were their most effective lures in different fishing conditions using my optical filters and knowledge of underwater optics. It was also very easy to predict which lures were ineffective in which conditions. Three problems soon became apparent.

Problem #1: Quality Control

Two lures that look similar in the store can look very different under water to a fish. These differences can take place with similar-looking lures from different companies and can also take place with "the same" lure from "the same" company. With certain types of fishing products, there is a real quality control problem when it comes to making a lure that has the same appearance under water. A friend of mine used my optical filters to test some fly-fishing material he had sold over the years at his shop. He had dozens of flies that he sold as Mack's Canyons. When looking at these flies in the air, every fly in the box looked the same. When he took the same fly and placed it under the green-water optical filter, some of the flies appeared to be multiple colors while others appeared black and white. People who bought these flies from him over the years assumed that they were buying the same product. He had no idea he was selling at least two or three different types of flies under the name "Mack's Canyon." How did this happen?

Lure makers dye feathers and fur until they reach a certain brightness *in air*. If the color appears a little off, some additional color may be added to "fine-tune" it. The dyes from many different companies may be used to get a final product. The problem is that these materials might look very different when placed under water. It is probably safe to say that this possibility is seldom considered or tested by any major lure companies.

Most fishermen fish by trial and error. How can you learn by trial and error when you do not know the underwater appearances of the lure that you are trying? Trial and error is very inefficient when you do not know what you are trying!

Problem #2: Improper Labeling

Numerous fishing products are not labeled accurately when it comes to color. Items are labeled "fluorescent" when they are not. Many items are not labeled fluorescent when they are. Numerous products are labeled fluorescent pink or fluorescent red when they are actually fluorescent orange. Looking at these products in room lighting in the store, there is no way for the shopper to determine which products have been improperly labeled (without special testing equipment).

Problem #3: Fishing Myths And "Old Wives Tales"

Many fishermen are secretive about their hard-won "fishing secrets." Many are not honest when it comes to describing them. Few fishermen have any scientific understanding about the effects of lighting on water. This leads to a large number of myths, "old wives tales," and inaccurate theories about fish vision that have become widely accepted. These stories can be a major barrier to gaining understanding about what is actually happening under water.

Breaking The First Myth

I read numerous inaccurate articles about underwater fishing lure color in the summer of 1995. I decided not to discuss these errors with the magazines, since I had not yet developed into a successful steelheader. From August to December of 1995, I began catching ten steelhead or salmon a month. I caught over a dozen summer steelhead from the Clackamas River, during a time that some local experts considered it devoid of fish.

My fishing success gave me the confidence to contact Nick Amato, editor of *Salmon Trout Steelheader* Magazine. My first demonstration for Nick, Frank, and their staff was well received. I then demonstrated my findings to professionals like Mike Laverty, Dave Schamp, Jack Glass, Bill Williamson, Bruce Harpole, John Beath, and Glen Young. Their enthusiastic reaction led me to apply for patents on the testing process. Over the past three years, this work has led to over thirty seminars, a dozen newspaper/magazine articles, three radio talk show appearances, a contract to design fishing lures for a major company, a side business, and the idea for this book. This information has been very helpful for me and I believe that many of you will find it valuable as well.

Section II
Scientists At Work

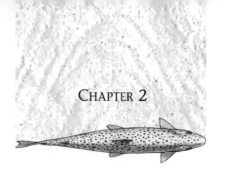

CHAPTER 2

The Early Research

EVER SINCE THE FIRST DIVER PUT ON A MASK AND DOVE UNDER WATER, people have been aware that some colors look different in water than they do in air. Photographers found a need to bring artificial lights to film fish and deep-water plants, because many things looked drab green in natural lighting.

Submarines

During World War II, the Department of the Navy decided that underwater color was important to understand. They attempted to find colors to paint submarines that would be visible in air, but have low visibility under water. Divers from the U.S. Navy Base at Groton, Connecticut, took a series of paint samples into water with different degrees of clarity to determine which colors were easiest to see under water. Divers concluded the fluorescent colored panels were the most visible. These researchers compared underwater visibility of fluorescent and non-fluorescent colors and found many different patterns in different types of water clarity.

Scuba Divers

These results were duplicated and reported by Paul Johnson in *The Scientific Angler*, Charles Scribner's Sons, pages 89-91, 1984. According to Johnson, "The non-fluorescent colors shifted drastically. The reds were jet black, the oranges were black, although the blues and greens showed negligible change. By contrast, the fluorescent reds, oranges, and yellows still glowed brightly their true surface colors."

According to the Eastman Kodak company, *The Fifth and Six Here's How*, Combined Edition 1977, pages 38-39, as light penetrates below the surface of the water, the colors of the spectrum are selectively absorbed. The blue-green color of the water is said to act as a filter, absorbing colors at the red end of the spectrum.

The Kodak article states the exception to the manner in which long wavelength light fades in deep water as being the case of some fluorescent dyes which retain their color regardless of depth.

Bureau of Surgery of the Navy sponsored a number of studies as reported in the *Journal of the Optical Society of America*, Vol. 57, No. 6, pp 802, 1967. Underwater scuba divers measured visibility of various colors, fluorescent and non-fluorescent, in four different bodies of water, which were set to measure a range from clear to murky. Studies indicated that various wavelengths of light were more visible in different water conditions.

Blue-green was seen best in water of good clarity. As the water became less clear, the optimum color shifted to longer wavelengths. The effects of lighting conditions, such as direct sun or shade, were minor when compared with the effects of water turbidity.

In very clear water, blue and yellow in non-fluorescent and fluorescent green and white were highly visible.

In water of moderate clarity, non-fluorescent white, yellow, and orange were seen, as were the fluorescent green and orange.

In water with a visibility of less than five feet, the colors seen best by scuba divers were white, yellow, and orange in non-fluorescent colors and orange or red in fluorescent colors.

The studies determined that fluorescent colors were always more visible than non-fluorescent colors. In addition, it was noted that certain colors that were seen tended to shift to the appearance of longer wavelength colors in increasing turbidity.

In his book *The Silent World*, Jacques Cousteau suggests that the angle of the sun over the surface of the water is much more important to the amount of light that penetrates the water to a significant degree than is sky condition. He explains that at midday, the light strikes the surface at right angles, rather than at a glancing angle, and that more light enters as a result of less reflectance. Cousteau also recognized that the sea is a bluing agent, which turns the appearance of objects to different shades of blue at great depths. Cousteau confirmed that at fifteen feet, red blood turns to orange, and at 55 feet becomes black (in sea water). At this depth, many orange objects also appear to look black.

Cousteau reported an incident where a fish was speared at 120 feet. The blood appeared drab green in color. As the spear fisherman returned to the surface, the blood turned black at 55 feet, orange at 15 feet, yet looked bright red at the surface.

Homer Circle reported in *Sports Afield*, March 1973, that at some depth red disappears and cannot be seen. Circle confirmed that fluorescent colors remained visible at great depth as the same color as they appeared at the surface. In clear water, non-fluorescent blue and violets were seen at great depth, although they took on shades of dark purple.

Paul Johnson's book *The Scientific Angler* included pictures that were taken in water over a hundred feet deep. This book included pictures of chrome- and nickel-plated fishing lures, fluorescent orange tubing, and fluorescent-colored fishing line, which all stayed bright at great depths under water. Johnson made observations similar to Cousteau's when he cut his foot on a piece of coral a hundred feet below the surface. He stated that a "green moss" appeared to tangle with his leg and that he could not free himself from it. As he came to the surface, the "moss" appeared to change to black, then to orange. It was only on the surface that his bleeding leg took on the expected "blood red" appearance.

Johnson also described his observations in a clear-water freshwater lake. He reported that bright non-fluorescent red paints appeared to turn a "dingy brown" at ten feet of depth and that at twenty feet, red objects appeared to turn black, and orange objects appeared dark brown.

Numerous articles in scientific journals have shown the light transmission curves of cloudy water from freshwater rivers and streams. These transmission curves show that color shifts take place much more in shallow water when the water holds more suspended debris. These studies show that in some muddy rivers, all purple and blue light is filtered out by water within the first two feet of depth. These charts show the reason why color shifts take place at shallow depths in water that has a greater amount of suspended dust or debris.

Underwater Photography

I am going to conclude this chapter with a series of photographs taken in air, in a swimming pool, in the waters of the Pacific Northwest, and off the coast of South America. I suggest that you turn to the photography section of this book and examine these 23 photographs (pages 129-143).

Pictures 2-1, 2-2, and 2-3 show a multi-colored plate in air and under water. Note that many of the bright colors in the plate appear to turn dark when viewed in a swimming pool that is only five feet deep. Most of us never fish in water that is as clear as a swimming pool. Most of us fish deeper than five feet. Significant color changes occur under water with fishing lures at surprisingly shallow depths.

Picture 2-4 shows a white plastic board containing spinner tubing, spinner blades, and red spawn sack materials. Picture 2-5 shows the board in 5 feet of green water in Washington. Even at very shallow depths, two of the red tubings and spawn sack materials begin to lose their brightness. Picture 2-6 shows the same board in 15 feet of clear blue water. At 15 feet, two of the red tubings and spawn sacks have gone totally black, while the one red tubing almost appears to glow.

Picture 2-7 shows a series of nine spinner tapes placed on a white background and the same nine spinner tapes placed on a dark background. When photographed in air, all eighteen tapes appear to be bright. Picture 2-8 shows the same board placed in water ten feet deep in the Pacific Northwest. Eight pieces of red spinner tape appear to turn black. Picture 2-9 shows the same board in 40 feet of water. At this depth, only four of the eighteen tapes remain bright.

Picture 2-10 shows a white board with several marabou jigs, an orange banana plug, spinners and spoons. Picture 2-11 shows this board at a depth of 15 feet and Picture 2-12 was taken at 25 feet. Picture 2-13 was taken at a distance of 15 feet. Note that several of the materials appear to turn dark, but that some color remains on the picture at 15 feet. Picture 2-14 was taken at a depth of 40 feet.

Picture 2-15 shows a red plastic board with an assortment of fishing lures. Picture 2-16 shows the same board placed in clear water 15 feet deep. Picture 2-17 was taken at 25 feet. Picture 2-18 was taken at a depth of 15 feet and a distance of 15 feet. Picture 2-19 was taken at a depth of 25 feet and a distance of 15 feet.

Pictures 2-20, 2-21, 2-22, and 2-23 are assorted pictures of the same boards at different underwater conditions.

I wish I had these pictures when the guide and fishing-store owner told me that he knew all about underwater color shifts and that they did not occur at depths of less than 100 feet.

As you can see from these pictures, water changes the appearance of fishing lures dramatically at depths of 5 to 15 feet. This is the range where most people fish. Except for anglers who fish surface plugs and dry flies, underwater color shifts affect the appearance of your fishing lures nearly every time you fish. Without an understanding of this information, you have been literally "fishing blind."

I believe that this is the first time that photographs have been published that show the affect of underwater color shifts using actual fishing lures, at actual fishing depths. Is it any wonder why fishermen are confused about the biting habits of fish? Why do fish seem to hit one color lure on one day and ignore it on the next? Before I attempt to give you the answers to these questions, I will first spend some time discussing water, optics, and eyeball structure. Refer back to the photography section often and examine these pictures. Understanding these 23 pictures will start you on the path of seeing *"What Fish See."*

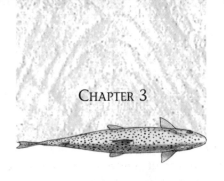

CHAPTER 3

Scientists Studying Eyes, Light, And Color

"...these lures are available in night-time fluorescent (finishes)."
"...a fluorescent element placed in the lure (to glow at night)..."

MANY FISHING AUTHORS USE THE TERMS "BRIGHT," "FLUORESCENT," AND "glo-in-the-dark" incorrectly. Many fluorescent colors are not bright, many bright colors are not fluorescent, and fluorescent colors do not "glow in the dark."

Optical Definitions For The Fisherman

Brightness: The ability of an object to reflect a large amount of the light.

"Bright non-fluorescent colors" reflect large amounts of the same color light that it receives. A bright non-fluorescent red lure would look red only if it is struck with red light. If it is struck with only ultraviolet, blue, or green light, it would look dark. A bright non-fluorescent lure cannot reflect more than 100% of the visible light that strikes it.

Color Shift: The phenomenon of objects apparently changing color underwater due to the light-filtering nature of water.

Fluorescence: The ability of an object to reflect light of a longer wavelength than it receives.

A fluorescent red object would look red whether it is struck by ultraviolet, blue, green, or red light. A fluorescent-colored lure can appear two or three times as bright as the visible light that strikes it because it converts invisible light (such as ultraviolet) and reflects it off as visible light.

Light: A type of radiation that can be detected by eyes. Light travels in "waves" of different length.

Short wavelength light includes ultraviolet, purple, and blue.

Medium wavelength light includes green, chartreuse, and yellow. Long wavelength light includes orange and red.

Phosphorescence: Continuing to shine in the dark after exposure to light; "Glo-in-the-dark."

Reflection: The ability of a material to return or throw back light.

Refraction: The ability of a material to bend light.

Scattering: The repeated reflection of light when it strikes small suspended dust particles.

White Light: A light which is a combination of all visible colors.

Light is a type of radiation that can be detected by the eyes. Light can be classified in terms of "wavelength." Different wavelengths of light result in different colors. "White light" is light which includes radiation from a variety of different wavelengths or colors. In order for light to appear white, it must include blue, green, yellow, orange, and red components.

Scientists Studying The Eye, Light, And Color

This next section is fairly complicated and some of you may wish to skip it. I suggest that you return to it only if you reach other technical material later in the book that you do not understand.

Scientists have learned much about vision by using four different methods:
1. Examination of eye structure.
2. Chemical analysis of materials in light-sensitive nerve cells.
3. Electronic monitoring of brain responses to light from different directions.
4. Study of animal behavior to light/food from different distances and directions.

Study Of Eye Structure

Many studies of eye structure have been done on numerous types of land animals and fish. Many types of animals have eyes located in the front of their heads, such as bears, cats, and dogs. These animals have two things in common—they all live on land and they are meat-eating hunters. Having eyes located in the front of the head allows for excellent depth perception, but a reduced width of visual field.

Other animals have their eyes located on the sides of their heads.

Examples of these are birds, fish, deer, horses, and cattle. These animals have one thing in common—a need for a very wide field of view. Birds and fish live in a situation where predators could approach them from literally any direction. They also need to navigate up and down, as well as from side to side. It is an advantage for plant-eating mammals like deer to have eyes on the sides of their head because it allows them to see predators coming at them from all angles.

The human eye is placed in a deep socket of bone and partially covered by the eyelids. This protects the eyeball, but also reduces the area of visual field that you can see. If you cover your left eye and look to the left, your vision becomes blocked by your nose. If you do not move your head and look up, your vision is blocked by your eyelids and the ridge of your forehead. If you look down, your vision is blocked by your eyelids and cheekbones. When you look to the right, your vision is blocked by the crease in your eyelid.

In the human visual system this protective bone structure results in one weakness—a very limited field of view. With the two eyes together, humans are able to see only about 180 degrees to the left and right. You cannot see things behind you and your vision is somewhat limited both upward and downward unless you move your head.

Here is an interesting experiment that you can play with a partner. Have a partner sit down and walk behind them. Slowly walk around them and look for the first moment that you can see their eyes. Tell your partner to tell you the

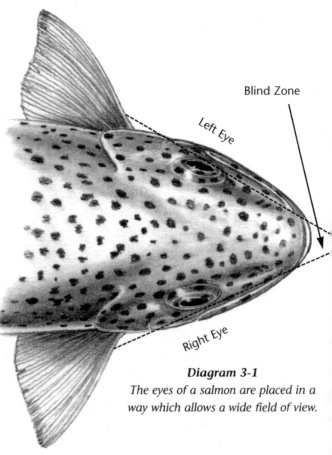

Blind Zone

Left Eye

Right Eye

Diagram 3-1
The eyes of a salmon are placed in a way which allows a wide field of view.

first time that they can see you. You may be surprised to find that when you see the colored part of their eyes is also the first time that they can see you.

Human eyes have a highly curved front surface called the cornea. Light enters the eye through an opening in the colored part of the eye, called the pupil. Any time that you can see the pupil of someone's eye, he can also see you (provided he has "normal vision"). This is true of most animals.

Look at Diagram 3-1, a drawing of a salmonid's head. There are no eyelids, forehead, or cheekbones to block the field of view. The eyes are located on the sides of the head and actually bulge out from the head, as opposed to being set in deep sockets. The cornea of the salmon eye is almost flat and the hole that lets in light is very large. It is possible for each eye to move in a large number of directions. When pictures are taken of this fish from the front, top, bottom, and rear, at least one of the eyes can be seen from nearly all directions.

Here is another exercise that you can do by yourself. Hold up a trout, steelhead, or salmon and turn it in different directions. Note that you can easily see both eyes when you are directly below or above the fish. Every place that you can see both of the fish's eyes are places where this fish has binocular vision (two-eyed vision or depth perception).

Scientists have used experiments to plot out the visual field of various types of fish. The visual field of a typical predator fish is drawn here in Diagrams 3-2 to 3-5. Fish have the ability to see with both eyes in a very wide direction. Binocular vision is possible both in forward, upward, and lower fields of gaze. Fish have a small blind spot directly in front of their mouth. This may seem important, but it is not.

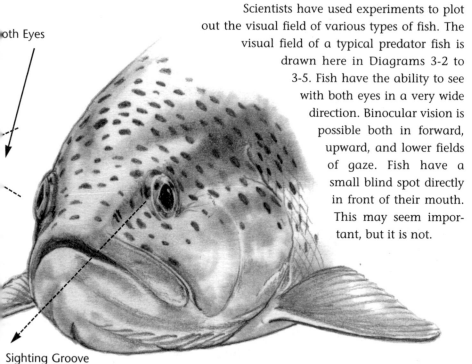

oth Eyes

Sighting Groove

29

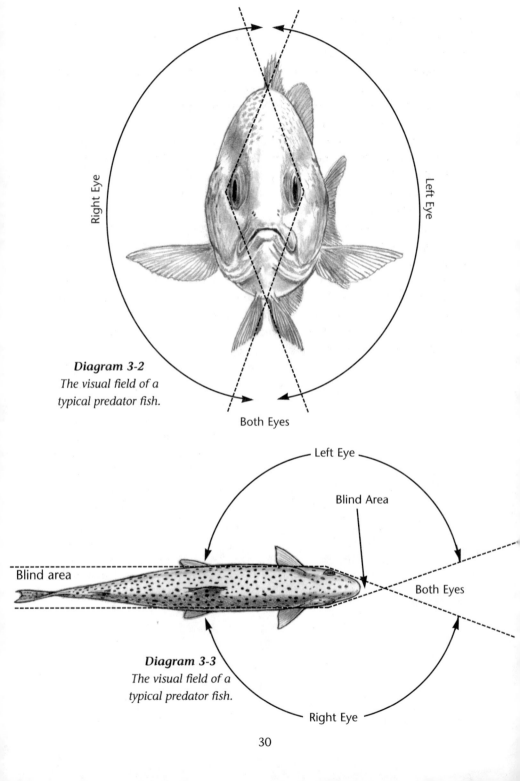

Diagram 3-2
*The visual field of a
typical predator fish.*

Right Eye

Left Eye

Both Eyes

Left Eye

Blind Area

Blind area

Both Eyes

Diagram 3-3
*The visual field of a
typical predator fish.*

Right Eye

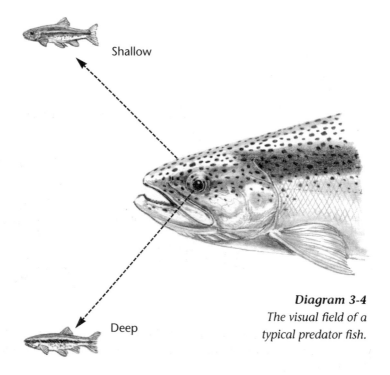

Shallow

Deep

Diagram 3-4
The visual field of a typical predator fish.

Humans also have a small blind spot directly in front of their mouth. When you are eating, you cannot see the food as it goes into your mouth, but it doesn't cause you any problem. It is much more important that you see the food 12 and 6 inches away. Once it gets within a few inches of your mouth, your hand should have no difficulty taking it the rest of the way.

The eyes of primitive fish (like sturgeon) are very different from human eyes. The eyes of advanced fish are somewhat similar to humans in that they contain a clear front window (cornea), a focusing lens, a layer of light-sensitive nerves (retina), and a variety of structures that detect light of different types—rods and cones. Fish eyes differ from human eyes in that they are more round, with a flatter front surface cornea, an almost round focusing lens, and the absence of a light-reducing pupil (Figure 3-5).

Chemical Analysis Of Materials In Nerves

Several key types of light-reactive chemicals have been isolated in the eyes of different animals and fish. Some chemicals react to small amounts of light and recharge slowly. These types of chemicals are important for night vision. Other chemicals are sensitive to certain types of light, requiring larger amounts of light, and recharges quickly. These chemicals are important for color vision. Some chemicals allow the animal to see red objects, while

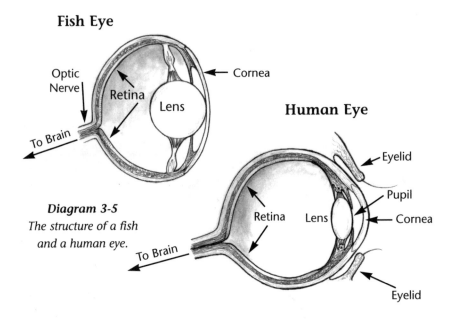

Fish Eye

Optic Nerve

Retina

Lens

Cornea

To Brain

Human Eye

Eyelid

Pupil

Retina   Lens

Cornea

To Brain

Eyelid

Diagram 3-5
The structure of a fish
and a human eye.

others react to blues, greens, or yellows. Without getting overly technical, the types of chemicals found in an animal's eyes give scientists a good idea of what the animal can see.

If the majority of chemicals in an animal's eye are of a type that reacts to blue light, then it can be assumed that the animal is able to see objects that are blue. If the majority of chemicals in an animal's eyes are reactive to red light, then that animal probably is best able to see objects that are red. I will discuss the types of chemicals found in fish eyes in a later chapter.

Electronic Research

Animals can't talk so they won't tell you what they see. This is true to some extent, but there are ways of getting this information. Monitors can placed above the visual portion of an animal or person's brain and experiments can be run to determine what things the animal is able to see. Small flashes of light, patterns, or objects can be placed in front of the test animal and any information traveling from the optic nerve to the visual portion of the brain can be measured.

Observing Behavior

The vision of many fish can be tested by placing lights, objects, or food in different locations and observing behavior. If a fish reacts to light from different directions, it can be assumed that the fish is able to see this light. If the fish can be taught to select food tied to different colored threads, it can be assumed that the fish can see these colors. If the fish can be taught to selectively strike certain colors of very thin monofilament line, it can be assumed that the fish can see both color and fine detail.

Using these and other tools, scientists have been able to assemble a wealth of information about how fish and other animals see.

Light and Color

Various types of energy from the sun hit us continually throughout the day. This energy comes in the form of electromagnetic waves. These waves can be classified by the length of the wave. Visible light is a part of this electromagnetic spectrum that can be seen by our eyes. The shortest wavelength that can be seen is violet light. Arranged from shortest wavelength to longest, the visible spectrum of light for the human eye is violet, indigo, blue, green, yellow, orange, and red. The light that is received through our eyes either comes directly from a light source (like the sun, a light bulb, or fire), or is reflected from the surface of objects.

There is a difference when we combine paints and when we combine lights:

Red paint + blue paint = purple
Red light + blue light = white
Red paint + blue light = black
   (non-fluorescent paints)
Red paint + blue light = red
   (fluorescent paints)
Red light + blue paint = black
   (fluorescent paints)

Mixing Two Paints

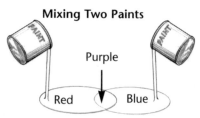

Mixing Two Lights

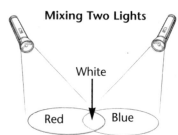

Mixing Light with Non-fluorescent Paint

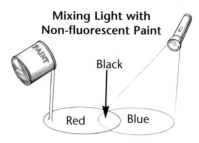

Mixing Light with Fluorescent Paint

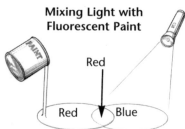

Mixing Light with Fluorescent Paint

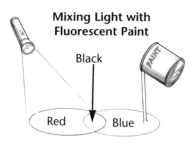

Diagram 3-6
Combinations of light and paint.

These color combinations are demonstrated in Diagram 3-6.

This is important because when we consider what fishing lures look like under water, it is similar to combining paints and lights. When we take a fishing lure into deep water, the light is filtered out by the water and eventually becomes almost a pure blue, green, yellow, orange, or red depending on water turbidity. If a fish looks at these lures in deep water, it is very much like combining a red paint with a colored light.

If the fish is far away from the lure, there is a large amount of water between the fish and the lure. The appearance of the lure is very much like what would happen if you covered the lure with a coating of blue, green, or yellow paint. This is what makes the underwater color of fishing lures so difficult to predict—we are combining lights and paints, paints and paints, or paints and paints and lights. Each of these three situations are different.

These types of changes are well-documented but they are things that the typical person never deals with because they look at everything in air through white light. When you go to a paint store and buy red paint it will always look red because you observe it through sunlight or through a white light bulb.

When you mix this paint with water color and different depths of water, it is possible to create the following combinations:

red + long-distance blue water = purple
red + long-distance green water = black
red + long-distance yellow water = orange
red + shallow blue water = pink
red + deep, green water = green

Colored lights mixed with paints, can create an almost unlimited number of combinations. These combinations can be further complicated by the fact that most light is a mixture of more than one color. Most "blue light" will also contain small amounts of yellow, orange, and red. When this type of "blue light" is placed on red paint the result could be that the paint appears to stay red.

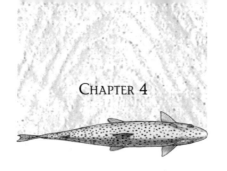

CHAPTER 4

Deep-Water Color Shifts

JACQUES COUSTEAU WROTE ABOUT AN EVENT THAT HE OBSERVED ON A deep-water dive. A diver speared a fish at a depth of 120 feet and what appeared to be a "green moss" came out of the fish. As the diver swam up to 55 feet, "the moss" appeared to turn black. As the diver came to the surface, the color of the blood appeared to change to orange, then pink. Only at the surface, did the fish's blood appear bright red. Cousteau observed the blood changing to five colors within 120 feet.

Point #1: Water filters out different wavelengths of light depending on the color of the water and the type of suspended material in the water.

Point #2: Water becomes more monochromatic (one colored) the deeper you go.

Point #3: Color shifts have been photographed in clear, tropical sea water at 20 feet. Similar color shifts take place in shallow depths in water with significant suspended material.

Mixing Paint With Colored Light

Deep-water color shifts are similar to mixing paint with colored light. Water acts as a light filter. The deeper that light penetrated water, the more "one colored" it becomes. In many tropical oceans, the light penetrating over 50 feet is almost pure blue.

Water's ability to filter out certain wavelengths of light causes what has been described as the "deep-water color shift." In tropical oceans, colors begin to change when divers go below 10 feet. In muddy rivers and lakes, color shifts take place at more shallow depths. There have been lakes where only red light was measured at a depth of three feet.

Paul Johnson (in the 1970s) observed similar color shifts when he cut his foot on a deep dive. He was convinced that moss was stuck to his leg, but he couldn't shake the green moss off. As he moved to the surface this "moss" turned black, then orange. At the surface, he realized that what he had been seeing was his own blood.

Non-fluorescent colors need to be struck with light of the same color in order to appear bright. Non-fluorescent colors act only as reflectors. Non-fluorescent red blood will look red only when it is struck with red light. When red light is filtered out under water, non-fluorescent red blood will appear black.

There is a difference between a "fluorescent" color and a "bright" color. Many fishermen use these two terms interchangeably. It is very possible that a "bright" color could be non-fluorescent and equally possible that a color that does not appear bright in air could be fluorescent.

Fluorescent colors are those which will continue to maintain their brightness even though they are struck with light of a shorter wavelength. A fluorescent red paint will look red even if it is struck with ultraviolet, blue, green, or yellow light. This is why long wavelength fluorescent colors are less likely to go through deep-water color shifts.

Fluorescent colors do not reflect off their color if struck with light of a longer wavelength. Fluorescent green paint will not appear green if struck with pure red light. For this reason, many fluorescent colors (with the

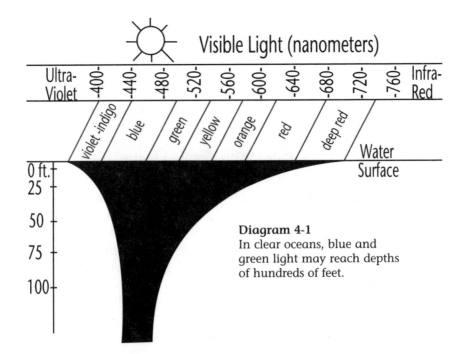

Diagram 4-1
In clear oceans, blue and green light may reach depths of hundreds of feet.

exception of red) do not exhibit their brightness in certain "muddy water" conditions where no light except red is present.

It is important to understand that many items that are labeled "fluorescent" are often a combination of fluorescent and non-fluorescent pigments. A "fluorescent pink" yarn might be a combination of fluorescent red, fluorescent yellow, and a touch of some non-fluorescent blue. When this yarn is placed in different water conditions, it might appear pink, orange, or purple.

All colors will eventually shift to match the color of the water at very extreme depths. But divers have observed that many fluorescent red and orange paints will hold their colors down to depths in excess of 200 feet, long after almost all other colors have turned dark.

Clear water, blue water, green water, and brown water will filter out light in different ways, depending on the amount and type of suspended debris in the water. Look at Diagrams 4-1, 4-2, and 4-3, to see light transmission curves for three different water conditions. As light passes deeper in each of these water types, light waves that are both short and long are filtered out. Light deeply penetrating water becomes "one colored." When light becomes "one colored" in deep water, the only lure colors which will remain bright are those which either match the water color, are white, or are fluorescent colors of a longer wavelength. All other colors will turn dark!

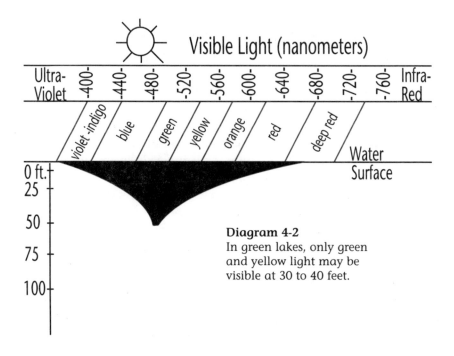

Diagram 4-2
In green lakes, only green and yellow light may be visible at 30 to 40 feet.

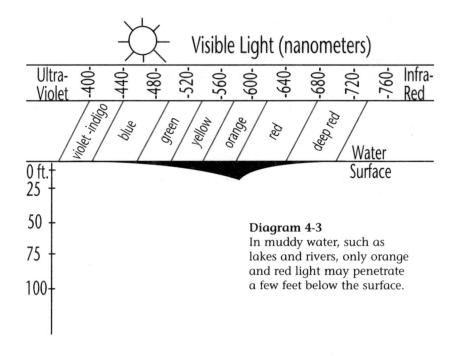

Diagram 4-3
In muddy water, such as lakes and rivers, only orange and red light may penetrate a few feet below the surface.

A Trip To The Swimming Pool

The owner of a tackle shop on the Oregon coast claimed that he knew all about underwater color shifts and that I did not have to worry about them unless I was bottom fishing at depths of 100 feet or more. He told me that there was "No way" that underwater color shifts could affect fishing in coastal Oregon rivers for salmon or steelhead at depths of 5 to 10 feet. He talked for long time about how he had "seen it all" and how he had caught thousands of fish in his lifetime. This was a very convincing argument and I thought about a simple method of rebutting his claims.

I knew he was wrong because I had done some swimming in the Nestucca, Trask, and Wilson rivers the past few summers and retrieved many fishing lures from snags at the bottom of deep pools. It was often difficult to determine what color these lures were until I got to the surface. These pools were usually less than 10 feet deep. I knew he was wrong, but not many people are willing to swim in the coastal streams, even during the summer. I wondered if a person could prove that underwater color shifts can take place in relatively shallow water using the neighborhood swimming pool?

I put on a pair of goggles and went swimming in our neighborhood swimming pool. Many of the children were playing with bright pink, orange, and purple foam rubber floating tubes (sold as "Noodles"). These are very popular and are sold at many toy stores. I have seen several anglers use them to make home-made drift bobbers. When I took a pink tube and a purple tube about a foot under water, I was unable to tell the two colors apart. When I took the orange tube down five feet, it changes from bright orange to dull brown.

When I dropped bright non-fluorescent rubber tubing or marabou jigs into five feet of water and began backing away, these materials rapidly turned dull gray. At a depth of five feet and a distance of ten feet, it was very easy to see the difference in brightness between the red fluorescent and non-fluorescent spinner tubing. Certain pieces of tubing turned a drab gray, while others appeared to almost sparkle. Many other reds appeared to turn orange or pink. Turn to Picture 2-3 on page 130 to see a picture of fishing lures in a swimming pool that was only 5 feet deep.

Few people fish in rivers that are as clear as a swimming pool. Most people fish frequently in water that is more than five feet deep. If you have a pool and a pair of goggles available, I would advise you to spend some time dropping different types of fishing equipment into the pool (hooks removed) to see what they look like under water at different depths and distances. Photography can in no way describe the difference in brightness that occurs when certain materials are placed in deep water on a sunny day.

Doing this exercise may give you some idea of what is actually happening in the underwater pictures shown in this book. If you are serious about your steelhead fishing, I urge you to spend some time sitting at the bottom of a swimming pool. Look around you and see how distant objects tend to turn a uniform blue. Note how it is difficult to determine the color of swimsuits being worn by some of the swimmers that are far away. Look upward at the sky, the sun, and note the difference in underwater brightness when you are in direct sunlight, as opposed to the shade. Look at how the surface chop distorts your view of people standing, walking, or sitting near the edge of the pool.

If the water is warm and you can hold your breath for a while, it is a great opportunity to study the concepts that I have put forward in this book. If color shifts can take place in a swimming pool in five feet of water, imagine the changes that take place in a typical cloudy Pacific Northwest steelhead river or stream. If nothing else, this experiment should prove to you that people like this store owner who claim that underwater color shifts only occur in 100 feet of water are not correct on this subject.

Fishermen are fond of saying, "Nothing beats experience." This is very true. If you want to understand what your fishing lures look like under water, all the fishing in the world is not going to teach you. The best thing to do is put on a pair of goggles and experience what things look like under water—even if it is only in a swimming pool. You can learn a lot about underwater visibility that many fishermen will never know. If you carefully examine the effects of swimming pool water on your favorite fishing lures, this exercise can teach you many important things which can help to make you a better fisherman.

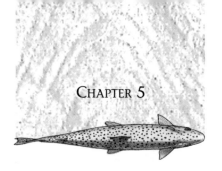

CHAPTER 5

Long-Distance Color Shifts

A SUMMER STEELHEAD SHOT ACROSS THE RIVER TOWARD A SMALL spinner. The fisherman braced himself for impact, but at the last instant the fish pulled back and did not strike. What happened?

Point #1: The brightest long-distance color is a fluorescent color of slightly longer wavelength than the dominant color of the water.

Point #2: White lures tend to assume the color of the water at long distance. In direct sunlight, white would tend to have greater contrast than on cloudy days.

Point #3: The brightest long-distance colors in green water are fluorescent green and fluorescent chartreuse. The brightest long-distance colors in blue water are fluorescent blue and fluorescent green. In very clear water, the brightest long-distance colors are white and fluorescent blue.

Mixing Two Different Color Paints

Looking at colors under water from long distance is similar to mixing different color paints. If you mixed red and blue paint, you would get a dark purple. If you mixed red and green paints, you would get black. Mixing white with blue paint would give you a lighter shade of blue. Mixing blue paint with green paint might give you a shade of blue-green.

Long-Distance Color Shift

Looking at these same fishing lures from a long distance under water is similar to the effect that you get mixing two different colored paints. Some authors have also described this long-distance color shift as being similar to

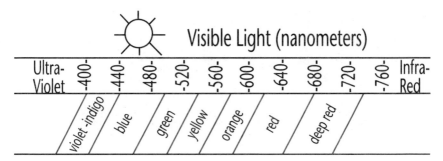

Diagram 5-1
Sunlight is composed of light of multiple wavelengths.

looking at things through a pair of colored sunglasses. Both of these statements are fairly accurate.

If you arrange a set of colors by wavelength, you would have a series of color bands starting with purple, and moving on to blue, yellow, green, yellow, orange, and red (Diagram 5-1). If you placed this display in water and moved further away, the colors most different in wavelength from the water color would lose brightness first. In blue water, the first colors to "disappear" would be red and orange. The colors that would be visible for the longest distance would be blue and green.

If you took this same display and placed it in green water, the colors would disappear in a slightly different order. It is likely that the first colors to disappear would be red and purple, with orange dropping out later. The colors visible for the longest distance would be green and yellow.

I sent some divers into the ocean to take pictures of a white plastic board with nine pieces of bright spinner tape. Three of these tapes were metallic, one non-fluorescent red, and five fluorescent. This white board appeared to turn light green at a distance of 10 feet. It was not possible to tell the difference between the tapes that were fluorescent, non-fluorescent, or metallic red, all turned dark. The orange tape appeared to turn almost brown, while the blue tape turned dark blue. The long-distance appearance of this board was very different from what was photographed in deep water at short distance.

At long distance, fluorescent colors may lose much of their brightness. White lures tend to take up the color of the water but are not as bright as lures that match the water color. If the water is blue and you view a blue and white lure at long distance, the white section of the lure will not appear as blue or as bright as the blue section. Thus a bright blue lure in blue water, or a bright green lure in green water will have greater brightness than a white lure—even though the white lure will turn blue or green under water.

Fluorescent blue, fluorescent green, and silver-plate are colors that appear bright from long distance in clear blue water. Fluorescent yellow, fluorescent green, and gold-plate often appear to be bright from long distance in green water. With very muddy water, nearly all colors will bleach out and appear to be the same. It will be almost impossible to see the difference between white, yellow, chartreuse, orange, pink, or red in muddy water. "Long distance" in muddy water may only be a matter of inches. In muddy water, the most visible long-distance colors tend to be black and gold.

When Is The Long-Distance Color Shift Important?

If you are fishing clear, blue water in a large pool, lake, river, or bay it may be possible for the fish to see your lure from far away. If you are fishing with a large lure that has some vibration, noise, or movement (such as a spinner or plug) long-distance visibility becomes very important.

Underwater bubbles, large boulders, and choppy pocket water tend to reduce the importance of long-distance visibility, since these obstructions will prevent the fish from seeing the lure when it is far away. The long-distance color shift is not much of a factor when fishing in extremely cold water since these fish are unlikely to take interest in a lure that is far away when their metabolism is lowered by the cold water.

If you are fishing cloudy, green water, a lure must be much larger in order for it to be seen at long distance. The long-distance color shift tends not be a major factor when fishing jigs, bait, drift bobbers, or small spinners in green water. The long-distance color shift remains a consideration in this water condition when fishing large trolling spinners or pulling plugs.

Long-distance color shifts have their greatest importance when using large noisy lures, in open clear water, with a water temperature that is in the fish's optimal activity zone.

What Happened With The Steelhead At The Beginning Of This Chapter?

It was a bright, sunny day in a large clear pool of water. The steelhead spotted the spinner when it was about 20 feet away. It was attacking a small red spinner when the decision was made to move on the lure, the spinner probably appeared to have a black body, black blade, and dark tail. When the fish got within 5 or 10 feet, the spinner probably appeared to change color to bright red. The steelhead "put on the breaks" and appeared to stop within two feet of the spinner, then swam away.

This color shift from black to bright red was unlike anything that the fish would observe in nature. Had the lure maintained its dark appearance for the entire distance, it is likely that the steelhead would have ended up on the hook. In clear water free of obstructions, with lures that attract attention from far away, it is important that the appearance of the lure remains fairly constant at all distances. I have seen steelhead do this to other anglers in the summer.

Moral of the story—stay away from bright fluorescent red lures in clear water, especially when fishing noisy spinners. How often does a steelhead move from 20 feet away to strike a lure? Not often, but it does happen. Out of the last 200 fish I have caught, I have seen perhaps five go from a stationary position, then move at high speed to strike my lure 15 to 20 feet away. On the other hand, I have seen at least twice as many summer fish that moved over 5 feet or more to the right or left to take a spinner.

I assume that each of these fish saw the lure when it was at least 10 to 15 feet away before making the decision to move to the side and take the lure. Even if the fish did not have to move to take a lure, a large number of these summer fish were probably aware of the lure when it was a considerable distance away. Throwing lures that do not go through long-distance color shifts greatly reduces the number of fish that appear to "dodge" your lure as it drifts down their pathway.

Before I begin to write about practical applications for this information, I need to discuss two other important items, the nature of water and how fish see.

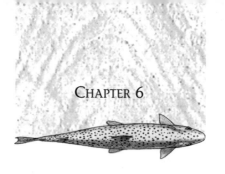

CHAPTER 6

The Nature of Water and Lighting Conditions

I CHUCKLED AS I SAW THE ANGLER CRAWLING UP ON THE BANK. HE HAD spotted a large steelhead and was apparently attempting to "sneak up" on it. I watched him for a few minutes and then moved upstream to work another pool. About 15 minutes later I walked back to the spot and hooked the fish. This angler had put so much effort into hiding from the fish that he had put himself out of position. I am certain that the fish was able to see both of us. In this case, hiding from the fish was far less important than putting yourself in proper position to make a good presentation.

Background Color

If you look at objects around you in air you will notice a multitude of colors. Objects do not catch your attention based on color, they catch your attention based on brightness or movement. Light comes from certain directions and these directions are easy to determine because it casts shadows.

Water is very different. In many cases, water will present a uniform colored background. Once you drop more than a few feet under the surface, the water appears to glow and light comes from all directions. As light travels through water, light is reflected and scattered. The more dust particles in the water, the more light is scattered. When a fish (or diver) looks at distance through water, this scattered light takes on a uniform "glow." The "glow" could be blue, green, yellow, or brown depending on the water clarity. It is a background unlike anything you would see in air.

When a fish or diver looks down, things become progressively darker. In deep water, things below you look like different shades of darkness, similar to what you see at night. With most underwater conditions, the only time you see a multi-colored background is when you look up.

When you look up, you may be able to see the sky, clouds, trees, rocks, and fishermen in various colors. You see this through a 97-degree "window" in the water above you. This "window" has been described in numerous

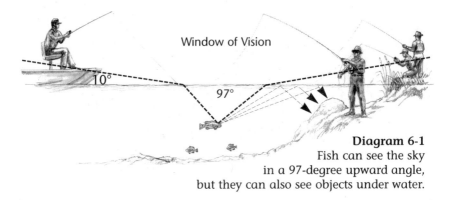

Diagram 6-1
Fish can see the sky
in a 97-degree upward angle,
but they can also see objects under water.

fishing magazines, often incorrectly. Because of these descriptions, numerous inaccurate conclusions have been made (Diagram 4-6).

Looking Up

If you are under water and look up, the surface of the water acts like a bumpy mirror. The word "bumpy" is very important. In a laboratory setting, with a perfectly flat surface of water, a person or fish looking up at the surface of the water will have a 97-degree window of vision through which he can see the sky. If the surface was perfectly flat, all you would see outside of this 97-degree window of vision is a reflection of the river bottom. If there is no river bottom (because the water is very deep), all you would see is a reflection of the deep blue or green water.

All the light coming on to the water from the sky is condensed into 97 degrees. For this reason, a dimly lit night sky appears very bright when under water. The dimly lit scattered light in the night sky is condensed into 1/4 the space. Underwater divers note that black fishing lures are easy to see against a night sky.

As light hits the surface of the water, some of the light is reflected and some of it is bent upward. If it hits the surface at nearly a right angle, it is barely deflected at all. The flatter the angle the light hits the water, the more it is bent. If it hits the water at about 10 degrees, it is fully reflected off. This optical theory has led some fishermen to the mistaken conclusion that they can crawl on the ground and get under a fish's "window of vision." They feel if they crawl on the ground a fish cannot see them. I will discuss this idea in Chapter 9, "Seven Underwater Fishing Myths."

If a fish is looking at a fisherman on the bank, the image of the fisherman is deflected so that he is seen somewhere between 45 degrees to 60 degrees upward. Light is bent in both directions so that if a fisherman sees a fish underwater, the fish will also appear to be "higher" or further away than

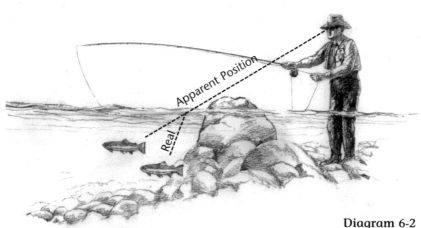

Diagram 6-2
Water distorts the apparent location of fish below the surface.

it actually is. If the fisherman is using a highly visible line, the line will appear to bend upward at the air and water transition (Diagram 6-2).

I have read a few fishing magazines that claim a fish can use the area outside its 97-degree upward mirror to see the river bottom far away. All this would be possible except that the surface of river water is seldom smooth! When fishing for salmon and steelhead, you are always in moving water, with some current and some surface bumpiness. If the ripple in the water exceeds 10 degrees (as it nearly always does), these laboratory theories are no longer valid.

There Is No 10 Degree "Blind Spot" For Fish Because The Surface Of The Water Is Bumpy.

On upward gaze, the surface of the water is bright and multi-colored.

Point #1: There is a huge difference in surface brightness as a result of direct sunlight as opposed to cloud cover or reflected light. The reason is that light from cloud cover comes from many directions and is largely reflected at the surface and does not penetrate. Highly directional sunlight can penetrate.

Point #2: Every break or bump in the surface of the water is seen as a bright spot from under water. For this reason, bubbly "chop" appears extremely bright from under water on a sunny day.

Point #3: You can see colors from under water looking up, but by far the brightest input is from direct sunlight.

47

So how would you describe the appearance of the surface film from under water on a sunny day? Every bump or bubble would have one side that appeared to be a very bright silver flash and another side that appeared dark. Filtering through this bright and dark pattern would be a moderately lit pattern of blue sky, green trees, white clouds, etc. These patterns would appear distorted and to vibrate or move with changes in the surface ripples. By far, the dominant appearance is the silver flash and dark pattern. This pattern would take place largely in a 97-degree upward window. However, if the surface of the water is broken, you will see intermittent flashes of the outside world right down to the shoreline. The pattern outside of this 97-degree window will be mostly a reflection of river bottom. It will tend to be somewhat dark, unless the water is shallow and has a light sandy bottom.

On a cloudy day, the surface of the water will be much less bright. Because the sources of light come from multiple directions, the brightness of the surface will appear much more uniform from under water. This moderate level uniform glare might make it somewhat more difficult to see objects above water. The overall color of the surface on a cloudy day would be white.

Using This Information To Select Surface Lures

For the fisherman, this information can be interpreted in the following way. In full sun, when a fish looks up on a clear river with a broken surface, it sees a background of very bright white with equally dark patches. Optimal contrast on the bright white areas is achieved with black, optimal contrast in the dark areas is achieved with white. Since the lure shifts through light and dark areas very rapidly, it makes sense to combine these two colors on a surface fishing lure.

On a cloudy day, the background is more uniform and moderate in brightness. The bright areas are still white but the overall sub-surface illumination is not as high. Due to the surface chop, some areas of the surface water will appear brighter, while other areas will be dark. Bright colors will give contrast to dark areas of the water. For summer steelhead, a good choice would be fluorescent green. For winter steelhead, a good contrast would come from fluorescent pink or red. White would not be a good color because it would blend in with the view of the clouds.

In the bright areas you want something that is dark like brown. On a cloudy day, this combination would give good contrast to fish that are looking up.

At Eye Level

At eye level, the appearance of the water will depend on how long the unobstructed line of sight is. In a large pool or river the background will take on the color of the water. In blue water the background will turn blue. In green water the background will turn green. The brightness of the background will depend on the lighting condition. On a sunny day, the background would appear to be bright. On a cloudy day, the background will appear to be dark.

If you are in a small stream or pocket water, the background will appear to be the rocks, logs, or river bottom that block your line of sight. If you are in the rapids, this background could also consist of suspended air bubbles. By looking at the shape or the river bottom, the color of the water, the lighting conditions, and the line of sight, it is possible to determine what the background appearance would be for a fish with a lure presented at eye level. As a rule, in big open water, consider the background to be a uniform color that matches the water color.

Looking Down

When looking down in deep water things appear increasingly dark and one-colored. Think of all things in deep water as being different shades of dark blue or dark green.

These different backgrounds affect the development of fish eyes. There are numerous fish that have different types of color vision depending on the direction that they look. This is outside the scope of this book, but some fish have color vision that works in the following way. When gazing up, they can see dark objects against a bright background. On a straight-ahead visual field they have their maximum color vision. On lower visual field, they have greater ability to spot low-contrast dark objects against a dark field.

Water Conditions

Let's backtrack a little bit and consider some common underwater conditions:

Condition #1: Clear Water/Sunny Day

If the water temperature is high, a fish may move into shallow bubbly "chop." Under these conditions, the white bubbles, being struck by direct sunlight give off an extremely bright reflection in all directions.

If the fish drops into the pool and looks upward, it will see a highly reflective, multi-color surface film, the white glare of the sun, blue sky, white clouds. This is one of the few conditions in river fishing where the fish can view a lure off a multi-colored background.

If the fish drops to the bottom of a deep pool and views oncoming lures at eye-level, then the brightness of the background will depend on the amount of distance between the lure and bottom structure. If the fish is near a rock drop-off, then the background will be dark brown. If there is a large amount of water behind the lure, the background will appear to be a uniform bright blue. If there is a shaded pocket of water behind the lure, then the background will appear to be a uniform dark blue.

Condition #2: Cloudy Day/Moderately Green Water

These conditions may take place at various water temperatures. The limited visibility will cause the fish to hold at moderate depths. The tendency would be for the fish to see the lure coming in at eye-level. On a cloudy day, the background would appear to be a dark green. On a sunny day, the background would appear to be bright green. If the fish sees the lure against a rocky background, the background will appear to be brown.

Condition #3: Muddy Water

During muddy water, steelhead will seek out water that is less muddy. They will often be found very shallow. The more muddy the water, the brighter the background. Because the fish are holding very shallow, this also increases the likelihood that the background will be bright. If the water is muddy, but there is direct sun, the water itself will appear to be very bright from under water, almost a milky white.

Reflected light has little ability to penetrate much below the surface of the water. By far the most important aspect affecting underwater brightness is the presence of direct sunlight. For an angler, the following general statements hold true. In direct sunlight, the cloudier the water, the more shallow the fish are holding, the brighter the underwater background. The brightest, most reflective background consists of air bubbles. Clear water, shadows, the absence of air bubbles or background rocky structure, and the absence of direct sunlight will cause underwater backgrounds to be dark.

Section III

Fishermen Trying To Use The Science

CHAPTER 7

The Physiology Of
Steelhead, Salmon, And Trout Eyes

I WAS FISHING THE CLACKAMAS A FEW DAYS AFTER A LIGHT RAIN AND caught several bright coho salmon on a green spinner. Later that week, I could not get them to move on the green spinner, but caught them on a fluorescent red spinner. A week later there were only a few dark fish in the system that would not move for anything until I shifted to my black summer spinners. This happened four times within a seven-week period. What was happening here?

Point #1: The eyes of Pacific salmon, steelhead, and lampreys contain a number of nerve cells with a peak sensitivity to blue and green light when in the ocean. When they move into fresh water and reach spawning condition, these nerves convert to a peak sensitivity to long-wavelength red light.

Point #2: The eyes of humans are oval and placed within a boney orbit, the eye socket. Because of this, the human eye has less than a 180-degree field of view. The eyes of steelhead are nearly round and placed on the sides of the head. This results in a field of view well in excess of 180 degrees.

Point #3: The eyes of humans are set in front of the face. This results in binocular (two-eyed) vision of slightly over 90 degrees. The eyes of steelhead are placed on the sides of the head. This allows the possibility of binocular vision both in front, behind, above, and below.

Point #4: Color vision sensitivity for many fish is different in different directions. Many fish have a different type of color vision straight ahead, than they do above or below eye level.

Color Vision

Steelhead have color-sensitive nerves in their eyes similar to humans. Fish tend to develop eyes that are adapted to the type of colored light they will encounter. Ocean fish like halibut have eyes that are sensitive to the blue light that reaches the bottom of the ocean. Fish which live in shallow fresh water (such as bluegill or perch) have eyes that are extremely sensitive when seeing orange and red objects.

Anadromous fish (such as salmon, steelhead, and lamprey) have eyes that are adapted to deep ocean conditions during a part of their life cycle. As these fish move into fresh water and prepare for spawning, changes take place in their eyes so that they are better able to see objects that are orange, pink, and red.

Steelhead and salmon that are in the ocean tend to have peak visual sensitivity to blue and green colors. Fish which enter fresh water but are many months from spawning, such as spring chinook and summer steelhead, may retain their green sensitivity for many months longer than their cousins that come into fresh water in the winter and quickly spawn.

Fresh coho salmon have a peak sensitivity to blue and green light when they are in the ocean and during their first few weeks in fresh water. As they develop spawning changes, the peak sensitivity of their eyes will shift to red light. Once they spawn and continue to change, their eyes will eventually break down to the point that they can see only drab brown and black objects against a light background. These spawning-related visual color shifts may partially explain the success that I reported at the beginning of this chapter.

These types of changes explain the lure selection of many expert anglers. Jed Davis says in his book *Spinner Fishing For Steelhead, Salmon, And Trout*:

"[For] spring chinook...I am a *green* fanatic."
"Green...is the best color for summer steelhead."
"Brown and black...are effective in dark post-spawning fish."
"Fire Orange...is my top winter steelhead color."

Why would different fishing lures be effective for different species (chinook, steelhead, coho), all in the same water condition? Consider the hypothetical situation that it is late August in a cold Oregon river. A small run of spring chinook have come up and are holding, waiting to spawn in November. Some summer steelhead are holding and waiting for January. Rain brings an early shot of coho into the system which come up and spawn immediately. These coho might be best able to see red objects, while the "springers" find yellow objects to appear brighter. The eyes of the summer steelhead might still be adapted to seeing green objects.

Even though all three fish are in the same river at the same time, the coho and chinook will be holding in deeper water where there is a greater likelihood that some deep-water color shift is taking place. For this reason, it makes sense to fish fluorescent red for coho, fluorescent orange for the chinook, and green or black for the summer steelhead.

Increased ability to see red/pink objects may play a role in spawning. These changes may make it easier for spawning fish to find each other and fertilize eggs.

"Steelhead And Salmon Can Only See Up, Right? ... Wrong"

This myth was probably developed by river fishermen watching fish come out of the depths to strike their lures. In relatively shallow tailouts and pools (less than ten feet deep), these fish may hold very close to the bottom. In cloudy water conditions, fishermen cannot see the fish moving downward to take a lure.

In order to understand fish eyes, it is important to have some understanding of human eyes and vision. The human eye is oval in shape with a heavily curved front surface (the cornea). This front surface provides 75% of the light-bending power of the eyeball. The human eyeball has a visual field of slightly less than 180 degrees because of the distortion of this highly curved surface, and because the eyes are set in a pair of deep, protected, boney sockets (Diagram 7-1).

The field of view of each eye is limited by structures such as the nose, forehead, and cheekbones. The two eyes are placed in the front of the head which allows for a large overlapping of the two visual fields. The human eyes cannot move independently. The disadvantage of this arrangement is that humans cannot see behind them without moving their head. Humans have several types of nerve cells in the back of their eyes that allow them to see colors during the day and to see in low-light situations at night (Diagrams 7-2 and 7-3).

The steelhead/salmon have eyes that are almost round, with

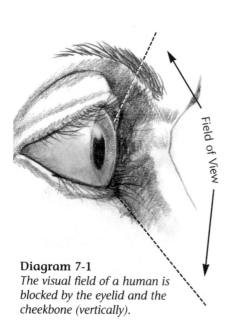

Field of View

Diagram 7-1
The visual field of a human is blocked by the eyelid and the cheekbone (vertically).

Diagram 7-2
The visual field of a human is blocked by the eyelid and the bridge of the nose (laterally).

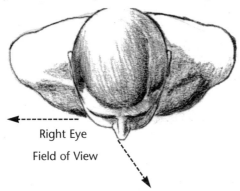

Right Eye
Field of View

a very flat front surface (or cornea). The flat cornea and spacing of the nerve cells allow each eye to have a field of view of over 180 degrees. The two eyes are placed nearly on the sides of the head, without deep boney eye sockets to reduce the field of view. Each eye can move somewhat independently. This arrangement allows for a slight overlap of visual fields when looking up, straight ahead, or down. There is a small blind spot directly behind the fish, but this blind spot is much smaller than that of humans (Diagram 7-4).

This ability to see in all directions is important for survival in the ocean. The only fish that are known not to have vision downward are bottom-dwellers like halibut. Think how difficult it would be for a steelhead to fertilize a redd of eggs if he did not have the ability to see down or backward. What do steelhead smolts and trout eat? Mostly bottom-dwelling nymphs! If steelhead smolts did not have the ability to see down, they would be unable to find these

Diagram 7-3
Even with the two eyes, the visual field of a human is quite restricted compared to a fish.

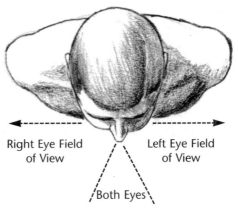

Right Eye Field of View

Left Eye Field of View

Both Eyes

nymphs and would probably die of starvation. The scientific research that shows that salmon, steelhead, and trout can see in a downward direction is solid.

Directional Vision

There has been research done on the directional color vision of many types of fish. I think that it is reasonable that such a situation also occurs with salmon and steelhead.

In humans, the greatest sensitivity for color vision occurs in the center of

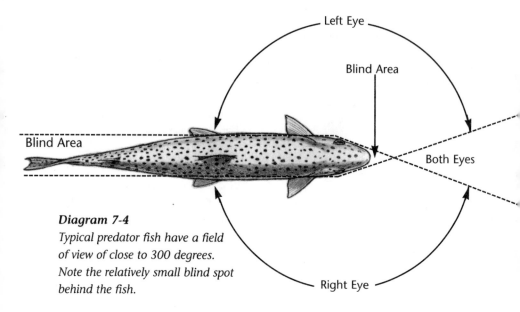

Diagram 7-4
Typical predator fish have a field of view of close to 300 degrees. Note the relatively small blind spot behind the fish.

our visual field. As you examine the parts of the eye used for peripheral vision, you find nerves that are more sensitive to movement and location. In many fish, the nerves appear to be concentrated almost in lateral bands. In the upper field, the fish appear to be best able to see dark objects against a bright background. In the central field, fish appear to have their best color vision. In the lower field, fish appear to have nerves which allow them to see dark objects against a dark background (similar to human night vision).

There are several reasons why I believe that steelhead and salmon may have a similar nerve pattern. In deep water, salmon and steelhead may suspend, holding well off the bottom. In some lakes, kokanee may hold hundreds of feet off the bottom, and similar situations occur in deep-water fishing for chinook.

I have talked to several fishermen who say that fluorescent blades usually produce the best but that there are a few cases where very deep-running nickel blades will be more effective. It is interesting to note that these fishermen have been saying "nickel" blades, not "silver" blades. These are experts and they do know the difference. It is also interesting to note that in deep ocean fishing, plug cut herring becomes more popular than trolling spinners.

I believe that these salmon have a peak sensitivity to fluorescent colors when the lures are presented to them at eye level. Under ordinary conditions they would be expected to take a large number of lures presented in this manner. Some of these lakes and bays get very high pressure from trolling fishermen and the fish will see large numbers of lures go by them each day.

They may become sensitized to these lures and eventually learn to ignore them.

The lower visual field of these fish may be similar to human night vision. Bright silver blades may appear excessively bright, just as humans find it difficult to look at headlights at night. The low reflectance of nickel will turn blue in blue water and green in green water. Similar changes will take place with the relatively low reflectance of plug cut herring.

My theory is that the success of deep-fishing nickel-plated spoons for kokanee, nickel-plated spoons in the bay for kings, or plug cut herring in oceans, may be, at least in part, due to fish seeing and striking these deep lures when they come to them at slightly lower than eye level.

I may be off-base with this, but I suspect that salmon and steelhead have directional color vision similar to other types of fish.

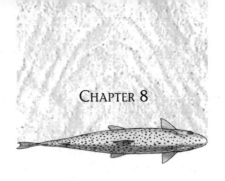

Chapter 8

Early Attempts At Using Underwater Color

DIVERS HAVE REPORTED UNDERWATER COLOR SHIFTS FOR NEARLY A hundred years. I know of only six major attempts at using knowledge of underwater color shifts to select or develop fishing lures.

The 1940s

Several fly fishermen reportedly used scuba gear to observe underwater bait-fish and how certain saltwater flies appeared under water. This information was used in some early designs for saltwater steelhead and salmon flies. These fishermen reportedly attempted to tie saltwater salmon flies that looked like underwater baitfish and even tested what these flies looked like under water. The long-term value of this project was questionable since color shifts vary with materials and dye lots, and this problem was never considered.

The 1950s

A piece of fishing equipment was developed which measured the color of light that penetrated under water. This instrument had limited value because it did not address what happened to specific fishing lures. A patent was issued and was apparently intended for bass fishing. This product never reached widespread acceptance in the sport fishing industry.

Also in the 50s came the development of the drift bobber. These small pieces of cork or Styrofoam were painted with fluorescent paints in all shapes and sizes. Over the years, many designs, such as Corkies, Oakies, Cheaters, Birdies, Pills, Spin-n-glos, were developed—all of which were effective. The common denominator of these lures is that they float and most are colored with highly fluorescent paint. Their lack of scent, chewy texture, and in most cases "action," did not detract from their effectiveness. The lesson learned from these drift bobbers is that fluorescent dyes are effective in increasing the "catch rate" of salmon and steelhead. This led to the use of fluorescent yarns and fluorescent dyes being added to roe cures.

The 1970s

A patent was issued on a piece of fishing equipment that combined an electric light sensor with a chart that reportedly determined which color lures would be effective for fishing that particular water condition. This instrument gained extensive popularity with fishing tackle companies interested in bass. It became known as the Color C-lector. In order to understand why it was effective in certain types of bass fishing (and less effective in steelhead fishing) it is important to understand how the product was developed.

It was based on an electronic probe that could be lowered into the water and determine the color of light that reaches that depth of water in that water condition.

A simplified description of their research is that they took bass and put them in holding tanks of different water clarity. They measured the color of light hitting each of the bass. They dyed food pellets with a number of different colors and dropped these pellets into the bass tanks, counting how many of each color pellet the bass ate. They repeated this experiment many times with different combinations of colored food pellets until they established patterns.

They concluded that for different types of water clarity, the bass preferred eating certain colored food pellets. This information was put into a chart. They assumed that bass living in rivers and lakes with the same type of water clarity would prefer to eat food pellets of the same color as those in the tank. The researchers recognized that different paints acted differently under water so they advised their suggestions would be valid if lures were painted with Color C-lector paints. Many lure builders embraced this idea and came out with lures painted in these colors.

Many bass anglers found this product to be effective in certain conditions. Some stores began to promote the product for fishing salmon and steelhead in the Pacific Northwest, but results for this type of fishing were not encouraging. There are several reasons why this product may not have been as useful for steelhead fishing.

It addressed the type of color food pellet bass preferred to eat in a tank. Steelhead, trout, and salmon have a much different diet from bass. It is questionable whether steelhead and salmon routinely feed in fresh water. They almost certainly are not attracted to bass pellets.

Color is taken up differently on a food pellet than it is on a piece of metal, rubber, fur, or plastic. Even if the lure maker uses the same dyes, the appearance on different materials is questionable.

Experiments were done in a tank. Underwater structure such as rocks, bubbles, sun, shade, and other factors definitely affect underwater contrast and visibility. An electronic probe measures light coming from all directions, which may be different from a fish's "line of sight."

The physiology and visual sensitivity for different fish were not taken into account. The peak visual sensitivity of a steelhead is much different than a bass. A steelhead eye is very different from a bass eye. A steelhead eye in salt water is very different from a steelhead eye in fresh water.

It measured a "feeding response," salmon and steelhead in rivers usually do not eat. They take lures for other reasons, such as being territorial prior to spawning.

It must be done from a boat or dock in which a probe can be lowered directly into the water. It cannot be done from shore, or lowered at an angle.

It does not address "quality control," that two similar looking lures can have very different underwater appearance.

This was a very significant device, which has considerable value within the limitations of bass fishing and the dyes or paints being used.

The 1980s

Paul Johnson's *The Scientific Angler* was apparently the first publication that addressed concepts concerning a wide range of scientific research on materials, line, smell, underwater color shifts, fish vision, and lure selection. This was a tremendous work, but contained certain errors relating to underwater optics and vision which were apparent to professional anglers, particularly in the areas of salmon and steelhead.

On page 103, he answers the question, "What color lure should I use?"

"(In coffee colored water)...start with brown toned lures."

"(In clear water)...start with dark purple...then work your way through the color wheel...blue, green, orange, red, and finish with white...think of fishing tackle in terms of defense rather than offense."

This advice was basically trial and error, but it ignored conditions like water temperature, lighting conditions, underwater structure, and the physiology of the fish's eyes.

In talking to numerous professional salmon and steelhead guides, their tactics for selecting lure colors fall into three basic groups:

Group 1 I call "generalists." They develop one basic color pattern that has worked in the past and go smaller in clear water or larger in cloudy water. An example of this would be people who use different sizes of a pink/pearl Corkie with green yarn almost exclusively.

Group 2 are "specialists." These people vary the color of the lure based on observations of water clarity, temperature, and species. Examples of this would be people who use large black/white lures in muddy water, large fluorescent red/orange lures in moderate green water, and dropping to smaller green or black lures on clear, low summer conditions. It is interesting that many people who use this strategy utilize black lures for both very clear and very muddy conditions.

Group 3 are the "switchers." They have a number of specific lures that have worked in some situations in the past. They randomly switch from lure to lure until they find something that works, without trying to reason or establish patterns.

It is interesting to note that if any of these groups are asked to name a starter lure for these three previously mentioned water conditions, none would follow Johnson's suggested pattern. I suspect that these suggestions are sound if you were fishing for bass, but not salmon or steelhead.

Johnson's book had a huge amount of information concerning the sensory system of fish—smell, vibration, sight, and taste. It had extensive information about underwater color shifts, reflection of light, and visibility. It remains one of the greatest books ever written about scientific aspects of fishing.

It was targeted largely at bass fishing and contained some basic misunderstandings about the reflecting properties of water. It has been highly quoted directly and indirectly in numerous fishing magazines.

The 1990s

The sixth major attempt to use underwater optics in lure selection will be described in this book. It takes into consideration underwater color shifts, background lighting, underwater structure, water temperature, lure type, lure quality control, fish physiology, water depth, water turbidity, and puts it into a system that can be used to select effective lures from any source or company. The process is simplified by a system of lights, optical filters, and backgrounds. I initially called this system the "Steelhead Color Selector," but have now renamed it the "See Best System (SBS)." Although it was designed for steelhead, salmon, and trout, it can be modified for other species by understanding the difference in sensitivity of different fish species to different colored lights.

The central thrust of this system is that all lures are not created equal. Three different materials dyed with the same fluorescent dye, can look very different when viewed under water. This program takes an "offensive" rather than "defensive" view when it comes to color selection. It suggests that there are specific types of orange, red, pink, yellow, or green dyes, which result in greater visibility in specific water conditions.

It poses a question that no other system has considered, the manner in which water affects the visibility of fishing lures. Fluorescent dyes increase the effectiveness of many steelhead lures in low-visibility water conditions. A problem results because having the label "fluorescent" gives no information about how bright the material actually will be when fished under water.

CHAPTER 9

Seven Underwater Fishing Myths
Or
A Little Bit Of Knowledge
Is A Bad Thing!

MANY ANGLERS HAVE ATTEMPTED TO USE SCIENTIFIC RESEARCH TO explain fish behavior. Incorrect application of the research has led to many faulty theories.

Myth #1: *Steelhead cannot see pink and that's why commercial gill nets are pink.*

At the University of Florida research was done where salmon were exposed to nets of different color. The salmon avoided the nets which were black, blue, or green, but swam into the nets which were clear or pink. The conclusion that some people might make is that salmon or steelhead cannot see pink. These experiments were done concerning fish that were in the ocean. It is likely that these salmon were sexually immature. Their eyes would still be in a stage of ocean adaptation and have a peak sensitivity to green colors. I would expect that a fish at this stage of its life cycle would have difficulty seeing pink objects.

Even if these gill nets were placed at the mouth of a river, it is possible that many of these fish would still not be ripe for spawning. If these fish have entered the river and made spawning changes, the peak sensitivity of their eyes would shift to colors that were orange, pink, or red. That is why the majority of all drift bobbers are pink or red. For spawning mature salmon and steelhead, pinks and reds are the easiest colors to see. This myth was the result of taking information from one period in the fish's life cycle and applying it to all periods.

Myth #2: *By creeping low to the ground, the angler can stalk a fish and get under its cone of vision.*

This is a myth that has been mentioned in numerous fishing publications. Many authors have heard that fish have a 97-degree upward window of vision and that they have a line of sight that leaves the water at 10 degrees

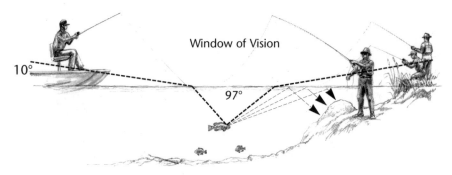

Diagram 9-1

Many fishing writers misinterpret the term "cone of vision" to mean that the fish can only see upward in a 97-degree field of view. If this were true, the fish in this diagram would not be able to see the bottom of the boat, the feet of the fisherman standing in the water, the fish in deeper water, or insects and nymphs on bottom.

If this were the case, it would be easy to sneak up on a fish by wading in the water or by boat...it would be simple for predators to attack the fish from below...and the fish would not have been able to feed (as smolt) by eating aquatic insects.

It is obvious that this interpretation is flawed. The term "cone of vision" does not mean that this is where the fish is able to see. It means this is where the fish is able to see..."with the sky as a background!" The fish is able to see in other areas as well, with either surface foam, dark river bed, or green water as a background.

(See Diagram 9-1). They have written that if you can stay lower than 10 degrees, it is possible for an angler to sneak up on a fish and cast to it without being spotted by the fish. It sounds reasonable in theory, but does not actually take place in real life. The reason that this theory does not work is that the river's surface is not smooth and river banks are steeper than 10 degrees.

Paul Johnson wrote about sitting at the bottom of a river in scuba gear and looking up at anglers attempting to approach the river in a crouched position. In every case, he was able to easily spot the angler by simply looking up. It was his statement that the only way an angler could approach a fish without being seen was to stand back from the river and make casts of 75 feet or more. Johnson wrote that he smiled as he thought of anglers who crouched down believing that they were invisible to the fish. He added, "if they were less than 40 feet away I guarantee their presence has been duly noted."

It is possible for the fish to see the surface of the shore itself if the water

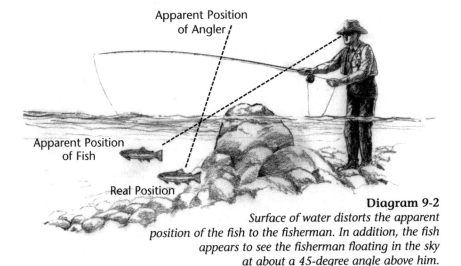

Diagram 9-2
*Surface of water distorts the apparent
position of the fish to the fisherman. In addition, the fish
appears to see the fisherman floating in the sky
at about a 45-degree angle above him.*

surface is angled even ten degrees in a ripple.

This experiment can be duplicated by sitting at the bottom of a swimming pool and asking some of your family members to try to sneak up on the pool without being seen. Every movement they make, even from a prone position is extremely easy to see. Especially easy to see are the arm movements of a cast, whether they are standing or in a prone position.

How did the authors misinterpret this "scientific data," and why do their claims not match the underwater observations? Apparently the fishing authors did not take the slope of the bank into consideration. The fish's line of sight is 10 degrees off the point where the light enters the water. Ten degrees is a very shallow slope! It is likely that the bank is much steeper than 10 degrees, making everything on the bank very visible to the fish, regardless of how low you go. Even though the fishing authors state that you could sneak up on a fish by staying low, in real life river banks have to be steep to hold the water within their bank. The main advantage for creeping is that you are moving slowly and not scaring the fish. They can see you, but as long as you do not move fast, they may not care.

Myth #3: *A fish can actually see around a rock and see you before you can see it.*

Scientific data shows that light bends at the transition of water and air. If light was leaving the fish at 44 degrees and struck the water/air surface, it would bend and leave the water at 10 degrees. Seeing how this light bends (Diagram 9-2), you can see how it is possible that a fish could "see around a rock." This is where fishing authors have misinterpreted the "scientific data." Light goes the same route in both directions! If the fish can see up and around a rock looking up, the angler can also see down and around a rock looking at the fish. The angler does not see the fish where it is actually located.

A more accurate statement might be that because of the optical nature of water, it is possible for both the fish and the angler to "see around a rock," and see things which would not be possible to see if the water was not present.

Myth #4: *Steelhead and trout are colorblind.*

This is another myth that may have developed because of fishing experience. An angler may note that on a given day black and purple lures work well. On another day, yellow, orange, or red are equally effective. In certain conditions under water, black does look exactly like purple. In other water conditions, yellow, orange, and red look the same. The observations are caused by a lack of understanding of the optical nature of water, not by a deficiency in the fish's color vision. (See pictures 2-1 to 2-23 on pages 129-143.)

Myth #5: *Polar bear fur is a good reflector of ultraviolet light. It is how it reflects invisible light that makes it an exceptional material for fly fishing clear water.*

This cannot be valid for two reasons. Ultraviolet light is filtered out by the depth of the water. Except at the surface, ultraviolet light will not affect the

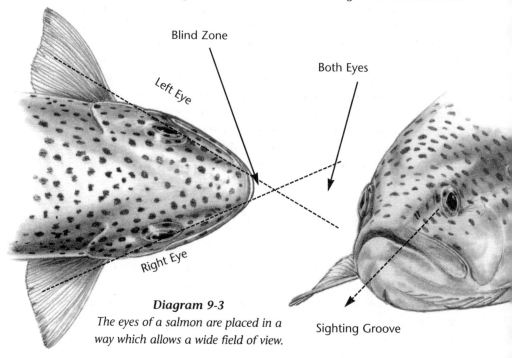

Blind Zone

Both Eyes

Left Eye

Right Eye

Sighting Groove

Diagram 9-3
*The eyes of a salmon are placed in a
way which allows a wide field of view.*

color of a fly in water. Second, even if ultraviolet light was reflected off a lure, it will quickly be absorbed by the water between the lure and the fish. Reflected ultraviolet light will only travel a matter of inches under water before it disappears.

Polar bear is still an effective material after it is dyed. Any ultraviolet reflecting properties that it might have would be destroyed by the dyes. The value of polar bear probably has more to do with its texture translucence and movement as opposed to any ultraviolet light reflecting ability.

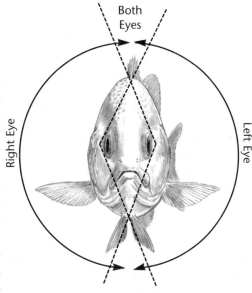

Diagram 9-4
The visual field of a typical predator fish.

Myth #6: *Our fluorescent line is high visibility in air but low visibility under water.*

A couple of fishing line companies have made this claim and it is not entirely accurate. If you take a bright red or pink fluorescent fishing line, it will look very bright in air. If you are standing in a boat and watching your line go under water the bright red line will soon appear to turn dark as it goes under the surface. The conclusion that you may make is that the line is bright in air but dark under water.

If you took the same line and looked at it under water the line would remain bright! A more accurate claim might be that the fishing line looks bright above water and dark below water (to an angler). The line would remain bright below the surface (to the fish). I suggest that this type of line might be an excellent material to use in the construction of flies and jigs since it remains so bright under water.

Many anglers have fished successfully with this type of line. This suggests that the importance of underwater visibility of fishing line may be overrated.

The advantage of using a high-visibility fluorescent line is that it allows the angler to see where his line is. This gives the angler a better idea of where he has fished and where he has not. This benefit may outweigh the disadvantage of greater line visibility.

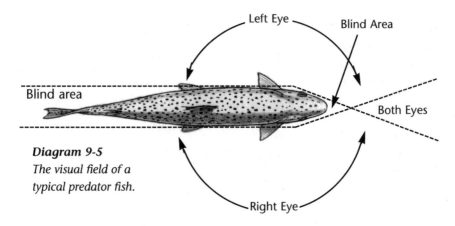

Left Eye

Blind Area

Blind area

Both Eyes

Right Eye

Diagram 9-5
*The visual field of a
typical predator fish.*

And now the big one! The biggest fishing myth told by Northwest fishermen.

Myth #7: *Steelhead have a large blind spot and cannot see down and/or steelhead have a "cone of vision" that allows them to see forward or up, but not backwards or down.*

This is a topic that I discussed briefly in Chapter 7, but I will now return to it in greater detail. This very popular fishing myth is the result of misinterpretation of the scientific data. Humans can see downward greater

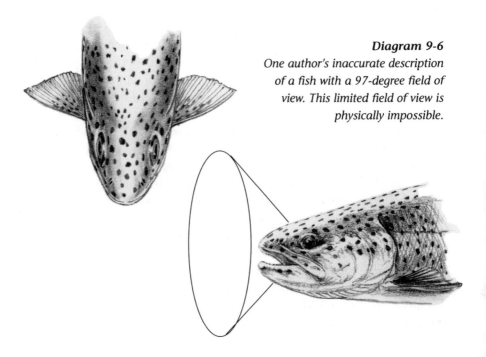

Diagram 9-6
*One author's inaccurate description
of a fish with a 97-degree field of
view. This limited field of view is
physically impossible.*

than 45 degrees and their vision is limited only by the depth of the eye socket. Steelhead and trout do not have this problem as their eyes are placed nearly flush with the sides of their head. Combined with the nearly flat front surface of the eye, this results in each eye having a significantly wider field of view than a human eye, both in the lateral and vertical direction. This vision in downward field is essential for being able to escape predators (Diagrams 9-3, 9-4, 9-5).

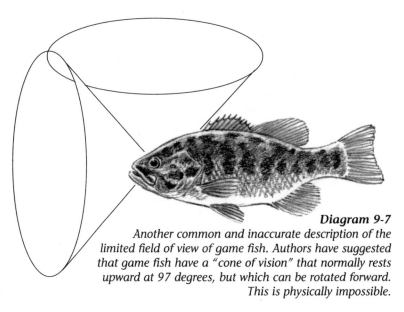

Diagram 9-7
Another common and inaccurate description of the limited field of view of game fish. Authors have suggested that game fish have a "cone of vision" that normally rests upward at 97 degrees, but which can be rotated forward. This is physically impossible.

I have read several articles that appear to be quoting statements made in the book *The Scientific Angler* when using the term "window of vision." One author wrote that a steelhead can only see upward or forward with a 97-degree field of view. Another claimed that a steelhead could only see downward if it turned its body sideways!

A human sees a field of view well over 100 degrees, even without moving the eyes. With eye movement, a human is able to have a "cone of vision" of well over 130 degrees, being limited by the depth of the eye socket and the bridge of the nose (with only one eye). Using the two eyes together, a human is able to have a "cone of vision" of between 130 and 170 degrees.

If what these fishing writers wrote is true, a fish (steelhead) is limited to having a cone of vision of only 97 degrees upward or straight forward, a cone that could be rotated in an upward or straight forward direction only (Diagrams 9-7 and 9-8)!

If this is true, the eyes would have to be tubular shaped (like a telescope) or set in deep protective sockets. These eyes would have to be able to rotate

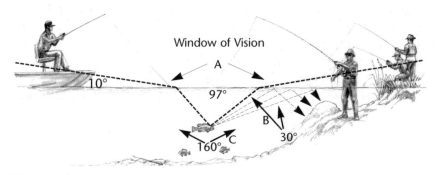

Diagram 9-8
Three "cones of vision"
Cone "A": The reflection of the sky serves as the background.
Cone "B": The silvery reflection of water back on itself serves as the background.
Cone "C": The dark floor of the river bed serves as the background.

in a forward or upward direction only. These steelhead would be helpless from predators like mackerel, sharks, or killer whales that would attack from below or behind. As smolts, these steelhead would only be able to feed on bottom-dwelling nymphs by swimming on their side to view the bottom of the river.

If this were true, then in Diagram 9-8 the fish would be able to see the 97-degree "window" looking up, but would be unable to see the feet of the fisherman standing in front of it, the bottom of the boat behind it, the other two fish swimming below it, and any aquatic insects crawling on the floor of the stream. It should be obvious to anyone who has done much fishing on a river that these statements are all false.

Have you ever seen a steelhead with deep-set or tubular (telescope-shaped) eyes? Of course not! A steelhead (and nearly all fish) has eyes that are much flatter than a human's and they are set on the sides of the head for maximum visual field of view (Diagrams 9-3 and 9-4).

A steelhead is able to move its eyes both upward, downward, front, and to the rear—with a visual field that has been estimated at close to 300 degrees (Diagram 9-11). Have you ever seen a steelhead move its eyes upward or forward? NO! When you observe steelhead in an aquarium, the eyes are almost always pointed either downward or to the side. With the shape of its eye, and the lack of eye-socket bones to obstruct vision, a steelhead can see a significant distance to the rear and below. We know that the steelhead can see up because we have observed them moving upward to strike a lure. Yet we *never* see a steelhead with the eyes pointing in an upward

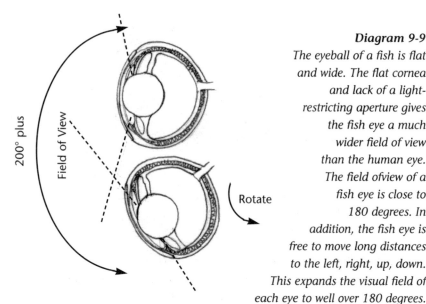

200° plus — **Field of View** — Rotate

Diagram 9-9
The eyeball of a fish is flat and wide. The flat cornea and lack of a light-restricting aperture gives the fish eye a much wider field of view than the human eye. The field ofview of a fish eye is close to 180 degrees. In addition, the fish eye is free to move long distances to the left, right, up, down. This expands the visual field of each eye to well over 180 degrees.

direction. This means that the steelhead has such a wide field of view that the fish is able to see upward without moving the eyes upward. This should give you some idea of how far to the sides and down a steelhead can see when it does move its eyes in those directions!

We will revisit the fish in Picture 9-8 and examine what it is actually seeing. There appears to be at least three "cones of vision" and they refer to the background against which the fish will view objects in the water. Above it, in "Cone A," the fish views objects against the bright lighting of the clouds and sky. Objects slightly upward (less than 40 degrees) are viewed against the bright reflection of the surface of the water. Objects straight ahead and down are viewed against the dark river-bed. As the water gets deeper, that color of the riverbed becomes progressively darker.

Diagram 9-10
The eyes of a steelhead or trout bulge out from the sides of the head. When viewed from the top, it is possible to see both of the fish's eyes. This indicates that the fish will be able to see you with both eyes as well.

The fish is able to see the outline of the angler against the "window" of the blue sky. It is also able to

71

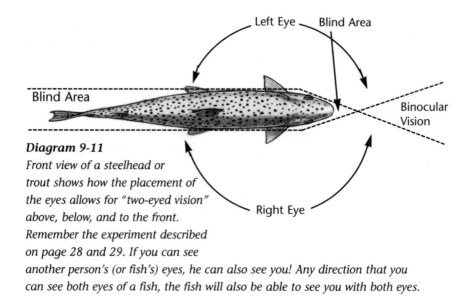

Diagram 9-11

Front view of a steelhead or trout shows how the placement of the eyes allows for "two-eyed vision" above, below, and to the front. Remember the experiment described on page 28 and 29. If you can see another person's (or fish's) eyes, he can also see you! Any direction that you can see both eyes of a fish, the fish will also be able to see you with both eyes.

see the angler's feet and the bottom of the boat against the bright surface reflection of the water. Aquatic insects and deeper holding fish are seen against the dark brown color of the ground on the bottom of the river. The steelhead is able to see forward, backward, and downward. Except for a small blind spot directly behind it (and a tiny one right in front of its nose), the steelhead has a huge field of view of close to 300 degrees.

Steelhead will attempt to swim away from predators that attack from below or behind. You never see a healthy steelhead smolt or trout swimming around on its side, looking for nymphs or aquatic insects in the mud. If steelhead were unable to see downward, they would have to swim on their side to fertilize eggs that are deposited in the bed made by the female.

I believe that the myth that steelhead can only see upward and have a field of view of only 97 degrees was based on misinterpretation of Paul Johnson's book. From fishing experience, observances of steelhead and salmon in aquariums, and scientific experiments, it is well established that steelhead (and nearly all fish) have a huge visual field. Their survival in the wild depends on it.

This is the *biggest fishing myth* I have heard among Pacific Northwest anglers. I have heard it from recreational anglers, professionals, guides, outdoor writers, radio talk show hosts, and professional fishing lure consultants. It makes no sense! It is a classic example of a little bit of knowledge being a bad thing and how difficult it is to dismiss a myth once it becomes accepted. Its only basis in truth is a misinterpretation of the scientific data.

I hope that one day I can put this myth to rest!

Section IV

Using The Science Of Underwater Visibility

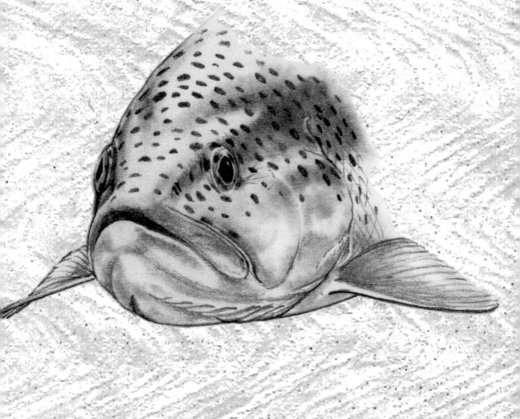

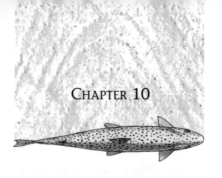

CHAPTER 10

The "See Best" System

"CHEMISTRY, BIOLOGY, OPTICS...THIS IS GETTING REAL COMPLICATED. IS there an easier way?" YES! I have developed a system that anglers can use to put this information to work. The "See Best" System is a simplified kit consisting of six optical filters and lights, which gives the recreational angler valuable information about which fishing lures to use in different conditions. With the "See Best" System you do not have to understand all the technical information or explanations. All you have to do is follow the Simplified 5 Step Process. The "See Best" System sells for about $60.

The Simplified 5 Step Process

1. Decide which of the six filters you are going to use.
•*What types of lures are you fishing?*
•*What type of fish are you going after?*
•*Will the fish be aware of your lure from long distance?*

If you are fishing for summer steelhead in clear water, pulling plugs, or using trolling spinners, examine your lures with hand-held "long-distance" optical filters and the "short-distance" filter/flashlights.

If you are drift, jig, bait, or spinner fishing in green or muddy water, use the "short distance" filter/flashlights.

•*What color is the water?*
  In clear blue water, use the blue filter.
  In cloudy green water, use the green filter.
  In muddy water, use the brown filter.

2. Decide which of the two backgrounds you are going to use.

•*What is the background?*

In direct sun place your lures on a bright-colored background, on cloudy or dark days place your lures on a dark background. Two backgrounds, a light sand and dark brown color, should work for most basic applications.

3. Split your lures into groups. Place all jigs together, all spinners together, all baits together, etc.

4. Put several lures on the background and look at them with the optical filters.

Eliminate those which have the least contrast. You should be able to eliminate at least half of them.

•*Are these fish "fresh" or spawning "ripe?"*

If the fish are fresh, then eliminate the reds and oranges. If the fish are spawning mature, then eliminate the purples, blues, and greens. If you are not sure, then retain the greens.

5. Take the remaining lures and look at them again under the same colored filter.

Which ones are the brightest and most visible? These would be your first choice.

Within less than a minute, you can identify which of your lures would be most visible given that lighting and water condition. This simple procedure with six filters and two backgrounds will give you very accurate information for most conditions.

If you really want to pin down the specialized lighting conditions, you might have to start combining the filters or use different-colored backgrounds. For most fishing conditions, this format will tell you everything that you need to know, it is that simple!

For advanced applications, read the rest of this book. But remember, this simple "one minute test" gives you a huge amount of information. It is probably all you need!

What do you do with this information? Organize your lures into different types—sunny or cloudy, clear or muddy water, cold or warm water, etc.

You will find that for fishing summer steelhead in clear water, a wide range of colors that look bright in air but turn dark under water, will be effective. For winter fishing in cloudy water, a small number of very bright underwater materials will be more productive.

You can still do "trial and error" fishing, but do it within the colors that tested out well with the "See Best" System. For example, you may have identified some lures that stayed bright yellow, orange, or red in deep, green water. The fluorescent red lures may appear to be the brightest, but consider using the orange or yellow lures if you are not getting bites.

What you do not want to do is randomly try the lures that changed colors, or that you know have poor underwater visibility for that color of water. The "See Best" System will simplify your lure selection and prevent you from wasting hours fishing with lures that are not visible for that water condition.

If you are fishing with effective colors and not catching anything, what does this mean? It is possible that either there are no fish present or your presentation is bad. Work on finding new water or improving your presentation, but stop wasting time changing colors.

I have met with numerous expert anglers and used this simplified 5 Step procedure. I was always able to pick out their most (and least) effective lures.

A fish has a brain the size of a pea. The factors that cause the fish to pick up your lure do not involve complex thinking processes. It is a matter of identification and action. Increased underwater visibility can translate to increased success once you have a certain baseline level of skill in location and presentation. Putting this technical information to work is both simple and effective when using the "See Best" System.

For professional lure-building companies, I have been using a more advanced version of this program. This system uses a professional micro-scope, advanced filters, lighting control, and a variety of other features. This system will give professional companies the additional information that they need to design different types of fishing lures. This professional system requires an investment in superior optics that would be "overkill" for the recreational angler.

For the recreational angler, practicing and testing your lures with the 5 Step "See Best" System will give you all the information you need to know. For proof of the accuracy of the "See Best" System, compare Picture 2-14 taken in 40 feet of green water with Picture 10-4 taken of the same board with the "See Best" Deep Water Green Filter. You will see that the two pictures are almost an exact match.

For further comparisons look at Pictures 2-6, 2-12, and 2-17 taken in deep blue water. Compare them with pictures 10-1, 10-2, and 10-3 taken through the "See Best" Deep Blue Water Filter. Again you will see an almost exact match.

This system works. By using the proper filters and lights, a person can predict the underwater color of a fishing lure in a wide range of fishing conditions. You do not have to dive under water or understand all of the science. It is a simple and quick method of testing lure visibility.

In the next few chapters, I will examine a number of successful fishing lures using this system. I will also discuss the unique problems of different types of materials used in creating fishing lures which have high visibility under the water.

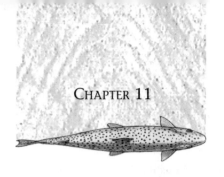

CHAPTER 11

The Drift Bobber

THIS IS A COMPLICATED CHAPTER SHOWING THE RESULTS OF TESTING four drift bobbers with six "See Best" System filters, and several underwater backgrounds. This will establish a pattern of how to test lures and how to evaluate them for different fishing conditions.

Why The Drift Bobber?

No lure can better demonstrate the importance of underwater visibility than the drift bobber. This classic steelhead lure can catch fish without scent, action, texture, flavor, or any other quality commonly associated with a good fish "bait." Effective drift bobbers can be found in all shapes, sizes, and designs. What most drift bobbers have in common is that they float and have fluorescent paint.

I have decided to limit this chapter to a single type of bobber in four colors, with no action or moving parts.

Two-color	Pink Pearl	(PP)
One-color	Chartreuse	(C)
One-color	Fire Red	(R)
Non-fluorescent	Black	(B)

Starting on page 147 are photographs of these drift bobbers in air and simulating nine underwater fishing conditions. These photographs were taken using the "See Best" filters.

The Conditions

Picture 11-1:   Drift Bobbers In Air

Picture 11-2:   Warm Clear Water, Sunny Day
   Filter #1:   Blue "See Best" hand-held filter

Picture 11-3:   **Cold Clear Water, Cloudy Day**
Picture 11-4:   **Cold Clear Water, Sunny Day**
   Filter #2:   Blue "See Best" Filter/flashlight

Picture 11-5:   **Warm Green Water, Cloudy Day**
Picture 11-6:   **Warm Green Water, Sunny Day**
   Filter #3:   Green "See Best" hand-held filter

Picture 11-7:   **Cold Green Water, Cloudy Day**
Picture 11-8:   **Cold Green Water, Sunny Day**
   Filter #4:   Green "See Best" Filter/flashlight

Picture 11-9:   **Cold Stained/Orange Water, Cloudy Day**
   Filter #5:   Orange "See Best" Hand-held filter

Picture 11-10:   **Cold, Muddy Brown Water, Sunny Day**
   Filter #6:   Red "See Best" Filter/flashlight

Summary By Color

The Pink/Pearl drift bobber appears pink/blue or pink/green with filters #1, #2, and #4. When tested against a dark background it is slightly more visible than against a bright background. With filter #3, it appears to be dark red/green, and is more visible against a bright background. It washes out completely in muddy water filters #5 and #6. If you were going to use one drift bobber all the time (except in muddy water) the Pink Pearl would be a reasonable choice. (Pictures 11-1 through 11-10, pages 147-150) By adding dark natural roe, its weakness in the area of bright blue water can be strengthened. By adding fluorescent green yarn, its long-distance visibility weakness in green water can be strengthened.

The Chartreuse appears bright with filters #1 and #3. When tested against a dark background, it is more visible than against a bright background. It had fair visibility with filters #2 and #4, and poor visibility with filters #5 and #6. The Chartreuse is better than the Pink/Pearl in warm water and worse than the Pink/Pearl in cold.

The Red had very good visibility with filters #2 and #4 and poor visibility with filters #1, #3, and #6, it had fair visibility with filter #5. The Red is an excellent cold-water lure but holds some visibility in moderately muddy water. It is a bad choice for warm-water conditions.

The Black was good in #1, #3, #5, and #6 and very poor with #2 and #4. This drift bobber is a specialty item—either very good or very bad. Its best applications are in warm summer conditions or in muddy water. It received the lowest grade in green water.

Summary By Fishing Condition

Giving each of the drift bobbers a grade of "A-F," with "F" representing poor underwater visibility and "A" representing highly visible. A chart could look something like this:

	Clear Water				Green Water				Muddy	
	Warm		Cool		Warm		Cool			
	Shade	Sun	Shade	Sun	Shade	Sun	Shade	Sun	Shade	Sun
Filter	#1	#1	#2	#2	#3	#3	#4	#4	#5	#6
Backgd.	dark	bright	dark	bright	dark	bright	dark	bright		
Cond.	#1	#2	#3	#4	#5	#6	#7	#8	#9	#10
PP	B	C	A-	B	B	C	A-	B	B	D
C	A-	B	B	C	A-	B	B	C	B	D
R	F	F	A	C	D	D	A	B	B	D
Blk	B	A	F	F	B	A-	F	D	F	C

Condition #1: Warm Water, Clear Blue, Shade

In clear blue summer conditions shade is not as dark as it is in the winter. The best visibility comes from drift bobbers that are bright at long distance against a moderately dark background. Chartreuse is the brightest. Since the background on a shaded summer day is only moderately dark, contrast can be achieved by either brightness, color, or darkness. For this reason the Pink/Pearl and Black come in as close to equal as a second choice. The Red drift bobber drops to last place because it shifts from black at long range to red at close range.

Condition #2: Warm Water, Clear Blue, Direct Sun

The same condition on a sunny day becomes extremely bright. Since fish might be expected to move to shallow, choppy water under the foam. I would test these lures against the brightest possible background. With these conditions, the Black drift bobber gives the greatest, most consistent contrast at both long and short distances. The Chartreuse drops to second and the Pink/Pearl to third.

Condition #3: Cool Water, Clear Blue, Shade

This is a typical low-water winter condition. The low water temperature causes the fish to be less mobile and the low winter sun, combined with clouds, makes the water very dark below the surface. These lures can be tested against a brown background. The brightest possible drift bobbers are the most visible in these conditions. My first choice would be the Red drift bobber, followed by the Pink/Pearl.

Condition #4: Cool Water, Clear Blue, Sun

On a cold winter day, in full sun, the underwater brightness is only moderate. The low winter sun results in light only a fraction as bright as a summer day. These lures should be tested against a blue background. This can be a tough condition where none of the drift bobbers show outstanding contrast. The best of the group would be the Pink/Pearl.

Condition #5: Warm Water, Green, Shade

These conditions are found on a rainy summer day. The warm water temperatures still result in high fish metabolism and the rain may add some color to the water. Even though the day is cloudy, the sun being high on the horizon still results in a fairly bright condition under water. Test this against a green-colored background and look for lures that give the best contrast at long distance. The Chartreuse comes in first, followed by Black.

Condition #6: Warm Water, Green, Sun

This condition would be after a rainy summer day. The water temperatures are still high, but the rain has brought some color to the water. The background will be fairly bright. Test these lures against an off-white background and look for the lures that give a consistent dark profile with and without the filter. The top colors for this condition would be Black and Chartreuse.

Condition #7: Cool Water, Green, Shade

This is the "classic" winter condition that many steelheaders consider ideal. Test this against a black background. In this condition, all fluorescent painted drift bobbers have good visibility. Whether you use Red, Pink/Pearl, or Chartreuse, all will be quite visible.

Condition #8: Cool Water, Green, Sun

On a sunny day in the winter it is still fairly dark under the surface of the water. Use the green background. The Red and Pink/Pearl are still very visible, although Chartreuse loses some of the contrast.

Condition #9: Muddy Water, Cloudy

Use a moderate-colored background such as tan. In stained water, the bright Red and Chartreuse show best. Black also gives poor contrast against the dark background.

Condition #10: Muddy Water, Sunny

For muddy water use an off-white background. Under muddy conditions, all colors except Black will wash out. This is perhaps the most difficult condition to fish.

Patterns And Conclusions On Drift Bobbers

There are several patterns that you might notice. The extreme "one-colored" (Red or Black) drift bobbers are either very good or very bad. If a person was going to stay with the same color drift bobber in a number of conditions, then a two-colored drift bobber in pink/white would be a safe bet.

If you do not fish warm water in full sun and avoid muddy water you could use a Pink/Pearl drift bobber and have a lure that would have good visibility for the other six conditions. By adding either green, white, or fluorescent red yarn, an angler could add visibility in one of the weak areas. A piece of fluorescent red yarn could make a pink drift bobber lure more visible in stained water. Adding a piece of green yarn could make the Pink/Pearl more visible in warm green water.

For summer steelhead on a sunny day, consider using a Black drift bobber, with natural eggs. When fishing on a dark day for winter steelhead, go with a Red drift bobber, white yarn, and fluorescent eggs. Each aspect of the lure—the drift bobber, the yarn, and the bait—can be considered both separately and together. If I were limited to two drift bobbers to use for all conditions, I would select a pink/white and a black with these two colors I would have something that would be quite visible under the full range of steelhead fishing conditions.

Bill Herzog has written that the only three colors a drift fisherman needs are pink, black, and white. I believe that this is because pink drift bobbers are made with paints that remain very bright in deep water. With other lures (and bait), this is not always the case. Silver would be better than white, but it is currently not possible to get high-quality silver finishes in drift bobbers. The metallic chrome finishes used in some drift bobbers do not come close to the brightness of silver-plated spinners and spoons. The performance of high-quality 24K gold plate also exceeds the brightness of "white."

Drift bobbers can be made with high-quality fluorescent pink finishes. I have yet to see a drift bobber with high-quality silverplate. This is the reason why the most productive color of a drift bobber may differ from the most productive color of spinners, plugs, jigs, flies, and other lures.

"Customizing" a drift bobber with a black marker pen can be very valuable for both bright summer conditions and stained or muddy water. The use of drift bobbers for steelhead and salmon remains a classic example of a "visual" lure. These lures are effective because they float off the bottom, and are painted in colors that are easy for fish to see under water. They in no way represent "food" in terms of smell, texture, or appearance. They are effective whether they are round, oval, tubular, or irregular in shape. Shape may provide some "action" in the water, but any shape will catch fish.

I hope that this will help to explain why drift bobbers are sometimes more effective than bait. Bait will almost never be able to have (and retain) high-quality fluorescent pigments. Dyes will quickly wash out and drift bobbers will tend to be much more bright in deep water. The advantage of bait lies in its scent, not its visual appearance. The advantage of live bait lies in scent and movement.

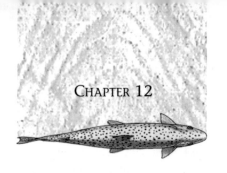

CHAPTER 12

Underwater Visibility Of A Steelhead Spinner

I FEEL THE TAP-TAP-TAP OF THE SPINNER BLADE AS IT DROPS SLOWLY toward a small pocket. It's like a count-down "3-2-1-zero-blast-off!" I see what looks like a submarine coming to the surface and suddenly my spinner disappears. The "tap" stops and I feel nothing. I rear back on the rod and see a three-foot-long summer steelhead launch itself into the air!

Catching summer steelhead on "trout-sized" spinning gear is my favorite form of fishing. For me, there is no bigger "rush" than hooking a summer steelhead on a tiny stream with equipment designed to catch eight-inch rainbow trout. During the past summer, I did most of my fishing with a 6'6" trout rod, six-pound-test line, and small spinners. I landed about 13 steelhead and over 200 trout each month.

Some people consider me a "spinner fishing specialist" and I really enjoyed writing this chapter on the underwater visibility of a spinner. I could have easily turned it into an entire book. I have broken this chapter into sections and will include additional information in later chapters concerning the use of spinners to fish for other species like trout, walleye, and musky.

Winter Steelhead Fishing: (Green or Clear Water)

Point #1: For winter steelhead (in green water) the most visible long-distance finish is silver. For this reason the outside of the blade should be silver-plated.

Point #2: The inside of the blade is seen from short distance. It should be the brightest short-distance color possible. The suggestion is fluorescent fire orange, pink, yellow, or green, some tapes are brighter underwater than others.

Point #3: The shaft of the spinner and the rear of the blade should be different colored so that it gives a flashing "strobe" effect from the side.

I have seen several winter steelhead designs that cover these three requirements.

Jed Davis Spinner: "The Winter Standard"

> Silverplate #5 body and blade, fire orange tape on the rear of the blade, and matching fire orange latex tubing on the treble hook.

Jim Bedford Spinner:

> Silverplate #4 blade with 1/8-ounce and 1/16-ounce brass body, fluorescent orange beads, two colors of fluorescent yellow tubing, two colors of fluorescent red or yellow tape on the rear of the blade.

The Dr. K Spinner: "The Winter Prime"

> Silverplate #4 body and blade, fluorescent hot pink/green tape, and "fiber-optic" orange tubing on the hook.

Using the "See Best" Green Water Filter, you will see that nearly all "name brand" spinners have non-fluorescent red tubing (on a treble hook) which turns black. I suggest cutting these hooks off and replacing them with a single Siwash hook and tubing that you have tested to be bright with the "See Best" Green Water Filter. I tend to go with Siwash hooks on #4 and #5 spinners and round bend trebles with my smaller sizes.

Test these spinners against a dark background since the sun hits the water at an angle in winter and little light penetrates below the surface. There are a greater number of cloudy and rainy days during the winter when the underwater conditions are very dark.

When you test "brand name" spinners, use the "See Best" Green Filter and see which blades appear the brightest. Silver blades appear brighter than chrome or nickel. Some silver blades are considerably brighter than others. You can also examine the blades with the "See Best" long-distance filter to see what they look like from far away under water. Blades that are painted red or orange on the outside of the blade may appear dark from long distance.

Put the "See Best," short-distance green filter light back on the spinner and spin the spinner slowly in your hand. What you hope to see is a "pulsing" of color as the spinner blade goes around the shaft. As you observe this, you might recognize that there are two ways of achieving this effect. The color on the rear of the blade must be different from the color of the spinner body. Either the inside of the blade should have color, or the body should have color but not both.

For shank tubing, fluorescent orange tubing is nearly as bright as red at short distance but more visible than red at long distance. Because of the cold water and low metabolism of winter steelhead, these spinners should be large. Most of my "green water" winter fish come on size #5 "Winter Prime" silver spinner.

There is an exception to this, which I will discuss at the end of this chapter.

Spinners In Muddy Water (Winter)

Point #1: The color of light passed by muddy water can vary from blue, to green, to amber, to brown depending on the amount of organic material in the water. Heavy glacial melts will filter out everything except blue, while large amounts of decaying plant material will filter out everything except red light.

Point #2: In the Pacific Northwest, muddy water becomes a red/brown filter.

Point #3: In muddy water, steelhead will hold very shallow, often breaking the surface. Because of shallow water in which they are holding, this must be considered a bright background in almost all cases.

Point #4: In muddy water, "long distance" may be a matter of inches.

The analogy that I like to use when fishing spinners in muddy water is that of driving a car on a foggy day. No matter how dark the day seems, the problem with seeing is that the brightness of the white fog wipes out all contrast. Consider how difficult it is to see a white or silver car on a foggy day. During a foggy day, what is the easiest color of car to spot? A black car!

Some people turn on their headlights while driving in the fog which does make them more visible to other drivers, but white headlights do not contrast well with white fog. What type of headlights are easiest to see in the fog? "Fog lamps." Yellow fog lamps!

In order to see something bright, it must be *very bright* and a *different color* than the fog! In order to get a better look at this bright object, it is helpful to have this bright target surrounded by something that is very dark. The best situation is getting something bright-dark-bright. Consider how easy it is to see a black car with bright yellow fog lamps driving through the white fog.

Using the "See Best" System, there is a red filter/flashlight which must be combined with an orange hand-held eyepiece. Test these spinners on a light or sand-colored background.

Nearly all colors, fluorescent and otherwise, will take on the color of muddy water. That means that nearly every color will take on the orange/brown/red appearance, regardless of whether it is fluorescent or not. All of these must be viewed against a white background, which will also take on the orange/brown/red appearance.

Silver will reflect all light and take on the same color as the bright background. A very shiny gold plate will give a bright reflection of slightly different color than the brown background. Two colors that give high contrast against the white background are dark blue or black.

Because of short visibility, it is important to go as large as possible. When fishing spinners in Oregon muddy brown water on a sunny day, I use a large 24K gold spinner blade with a heavy black body and chartreuse tubing. In the rear of the blade, I combine black and fluorescent chartreuse tape. I call this spinner "Down and Dirty."

Using the "See Best" Muddy Water Filters, you will see that the greatest contrast is achieved with spinner bodies of the blackest possible material.

It is important to realize that in muddy water conditions visibility with even the highest contrast colors may be less than 12 inches. Consider the value of different colors to be something like a "sphere of attraction." If a gold and black lure came within 12 inches in certain muddy waters, a fish might be able to see it. If the lure was colored silver, it might have to pass within 6 inches of the fish before it is seen. This extra fraction of a second might be the difference between the fish striking the lure or ignoring it. A fish might take either lure if it hits it in the face, but the optimal color might increase your margin of error by a few inches.

It might be possible to catch a steelhead in muddy water with a silver and red spinner, but a larger black and gold spinner will be visible consistently from a greater distance. Even with the optimal color combination in muddy water, the distance that the lure is visible might not come close to the distance that it would be seen in green water.

The spinner fisherman should look for small pockets of slower-moving water (often close to shore) that may contain less silt. When spinner fishing, I usually hit an area quickly, cover it with 4 to 6 casts, then move on. High water will reduce the number of places that steelhead hold, as well as limit access for the bank angler. Fish are often on the move, moving quickly from one limited holding area to another. For these reasons, I will often change my pattern and rotate between 3 or 4 prime high-water holding areas when fishing this type of water. It is not unusual to work a muddy pocket with dozens of casts before getting a strike, either because fish moving into the area were not able to see the initial casts, or they are not aggressively striking.

Under these conditions, I am often looking for pockets that are only a few square feet, and are best covered with short underhand flip casts of less than 15 feet. While I might cover several miles of river fishing on some days, I often limit myself to a few hundred yards and 3 or 4 prime pockets when fishing high-water conditions, rotating between the pockets every few minutes.

Spinner Fishing In Summer

Point #1: Spinner selection for summer is very simple. It essentially involves an understanding of underwater background and long-distance color shift. If there is direct sun, consider the background a combination of bright and dark. If there is no direct sun, consider the background to be dark. Test only for the long-distance color shift.

Point #2: Summer steelhead spinners are small, trout-sized #1,#2, and #3. Keep your spinners small and dark or a combination of small, light, and dark.

Point #3: Any color that goes through a long-distance color shift should be avoided.

I believe that four basic spinner color combinations are all that I need to be successful fishing for summer steelhead on Oregon streams. You can use the "See Best" System, Blue Long-Distance Filter to determine what you should not use. Test your spinners with a "See Best" Long-Distance Blue Filter and two backgrounds. I recommend you use a light blue piece of paper for cloudy days and crumpled aluminum foil to simulate sunny days.

By using the "See Best" deep-water filters, you will see that purple, orange, and red appear to turn dark. If the background is dark blue, then blue lures will be difficult to see. If it is a bright sunny day against a bright white sun, white will be difficult to see.

This testing indicates that black, yellow, gold, green, and tan give the best visibility on bright sunny days in clear blue water. On spinners, these colors are achieved by painting, tarnishing, or using pressure sensitive tape on brass spinner parts, or by using 24K gold components. The green can also be added in the form of tubing that is placed on the hook. Certain types of green give better underwater contrast against darker summer backgrounds.

My four favorite color combinations for summer steelhead are:

Summer Heat: A #2 spinner with a metallic brown blade and a black body. "Summer Heat" is used from mid-morning to mid-afternoon on hot summer days, in direct sun, when summer steelhead rivers are low and clear. The Summer Heat is also an excellent spinner to use for winter steelhead when the water is low, when fishing pressure is high, the water is over 43 degrees, and there is direct sun on the water. This is also my most effective spinner for fishing trout in the summer.

Summer Rain: A #3 spinner with a gold blade and a brass body, using fluorescent green/black tape on the blade and green tubing on the hook shank. "Summer Rain" is used on cloudy summer days when the water has a slight color to it. The Summer Rain is also a great spinner to use in the winter when the water is in the mid-40s, low/clear, and in direct sun. It is an outstanding lure to use on cloudy days for fresh fall coho and spring chinook. It is probably the most "multi-use" spinner that I have ever used.

Summer Deep: A #3 spinner that is similar to the Summer Rain, except I make it with a heavyweight body to work in deep pools. With the #3 Summer Rain, my bodies weigh about 1/8 of an ounce. With the Summer Deep, the body is almost twice as heavy.

First Light: #2 or #3 silver-bladed spinner with black tape and tiny glow accents, and a black body. The "First Light" is the spinner I use at sunrise. It can also be used in other conditions where the water is very dark. I like it on dark, cloudy days, where I am fishing areas in full shade. In a size 5, it can also be used in similar lighting conditions during the winter. I know many steelheaders who fish different sizes of a spinner that looks similar to this, for all conditions, all types of fish, all times of the year. I would say that it is nearly as valuable a multi-use spinner as the Summer Rain.

If I was limited to one spinner for summer steelhead and trout, it would be Summer Heat in a size #2.

If I was limited to one spinner for use with spring chinook, summer steelhead, winter steelhead, and fall coho, it would be either a Summer Rain or a First Light in size #3.

I have a few thoughts about steelhead spinner-fishing techniques. Most people fish a spinner too quickly. If I am catching an excessive number of trout, I will slow down the retrieve slightly and fish deeper. I tend to fish spinners with minimal retrieving, making adjustments in the angle of the cast to reach this goal. The ideal cast for me is slightly upstream, where the slack can be drawn in then let back out as the spinner passes you. If the spinner can go downstream in the bottom third of the river depth and swing with little or no retrieving (without snagging bottom), then I have achieved my goal. This results in minimal drag, good depth, and a very slow-spinning spinner.

The Summer Heat Spinner

This has been my most effective lure during August and September on sunny days for summer steelhead. It works best between 9:00 a.m. and 3:00 p.m. in direct sunlight on rivers with a water temperature between 55-65 degrees. It is very productive in pocket water at the head of a drift, and is exceptional on steelhead that are buried at the bottom of a big pool. It has better long-distance visibility against a dark background than an all-black spinner. Its dark profile gives it excellent visibility against bright underwater bubbles that are reflecting direct sunlight.

I prefer to fish the Summer Heat with a trout-sized rod and six-pound-test line. From the standpoint of underwater visibility, a black body makes more sense than a black blade. I build this spinner using a 1/8-ounce black body (in white water) or a 3/16-ounce black body (for large pools). I found that with the ultralight equipment, I could get by reducing the gap on my hooks. This allows me to lose fewer spinners to snags and to catch a larger number of "accidental" trout. With this combination, I have only lost one steelhead in over two years.

Davis and other spinner experts often tarnish their brass blades for summer steelhead. Jed has written that he carries the brass blades in his pockets for a few weeks or rolls them around in wet mud and sets them in an open can for a few months. There are better ways of doing this, especially if you are in a hurry to start fishing. I have come upon a number of excellent "secret sauce" preparations for tarnishing brass blades. There are combinations you can make using brine, film developing chemicals, coffee grounds, or contact lens disinfecting solutions, that do a beautiful job of tarnishing brass blades in a matter of hours.

Just as important as the "secret sauce" is the type of brass blade you use. It is very important that you use a non-coated brass blade. I found that the "electric brass" Pen Tac blade did not tarnish, and that the "plain brass" Pen Tac blade will take on only a moderate tarnish before developing what looked like raised "rust spots."

This is a common problem with "high-quality" brass blades, they tend not to tarnish evenly in "secret sauce." There are some relatively cheap brass "French blades" that will tarnish to a beautiful swirling brown finish within an hour of soaking in "secret sauce." I was unhappy when one company "upgraded" their brass blades so now they no longer tarnish to a dark swirl pattern.

I suggest that you buy blades from a number of sources and test them to find which brand tarnishes the darkest, with the best pattern. Once you identify some blades that tarnish properly, buy at least a year's supply. Finding blades that tarnish properly has been a problem.

The best "secret sauces" I have found for this purpose are saline and peroxide solutions designed for use in the disinfecting soft contact lenses. These include preparations like AOSept™ and Oxysept™. These are relatively expensive, but being an optometrist, I am able to get free samples. These products are the easiest and most consistent to use.

The Summer Heat spinner that I use has a metallic brown French blade in a #2 brass blade and a #3 black body. It is a very simple-looking pattern, but gives great visibility in clear water conditions in direct sunlight. I have had at least a dozen days in the past two years where I have accidentally caught in excess of 50 trout a day with it, while in pursuit of summer steelhead. It works great on summer steelhead, coho, trout, and (unfortunately) spawned-out, old dark spring chinook.

If your brass blades become excessively tarnished, you can often lighten them by wiping them with a Q-tip soaked in vinegar.

If you want to make your own "secret sauce" preparation for tarnishing blades, try this recipe. Mix half a spoon of table salt into a fresh bottle of hydrogen peroxide. Let stand for 15 minutes, shake well, wait about a minute, then pour it 3/4-inch deep in a flat glass bowl. Make sure that you do not accidentally pour out any salt crystals. Arrange the brass spinner blades one layer thick on the bottom of the bowl, do not stack. Keep spinner blades all rounded-side up. If there are any grains of salt at the bottom of the bowl, the blades will tarnish faster on the bottom and acquire a rough, raised "rusted" appearance.

Depending on the type of brass blade, you will need to let this solution stand for a period of time. Some brass blades will turn almost black within an hour, while coated brass blades might not tarnish even after a two-day soak. What you want is a brass blade that will tarnish quickly and smoothly.

Many brass blades develop raised spots that look like rust when soaked in this solution. I don't know the reason for this, perhaps the blades are plated. Here is a way of getting around that problem. Moisten the blades, place them in a flat glass or plastic dish, raised side up. Sprinkle the blades with a thin layer of table salt. Allow the blades to dry overnight and the salt to crystallize on the blade. Look at the blades through the salt and remove the ones that are starting to slightly yellow. Leave the rest, sprinkle again with water, and leave for a second day.

Take the blades that look like they are yellowing and place them in another glass or plastic dish and set them raised side up. Cover them with about 1/4 inch of hydrogen peroxide. The blades will start rapidly steaming and may get quite hot. Within 2 or 3 minutes, the blades are usually ready—just remove and rinse. Leaving the blades in for longer will not usually result in a darker blade and may cut into the base metal enough to make the blades start turning green. Remove them as soon as they darken, rinse and dry.

There are three problems with tarnished brass:

1. It requires some extra work.
2. Many blades do not tarnish consistently.
3. They look ugly.

I have been discussing these problems with a major lure company and hope to develop a plating processes that will deliver this finish, yet be attractive enough that anglers will want to purchase it. When this type of finish is done properly, I haven't seen anything that could beat it for summer steelhead or trout. Most tarnished brass that I have seen appears "flat." The most effective tarnished brass blades that I have ever made are dark with tiny bright flecks of reflective material.

These blades are also very effective for trout and winter steelhead. During January of 1997, the Summer Heat in size #2 was my top producer for winter steelhead during a high-water month.

What's Actually Happening Under Water

I have never read anyone trying to describe what actually happens to a steelhead spinner when it is thrown into the water. Since this book is entitled *What Fish See*, I have decided to describe how a fish might see a spinner.

In the "basic swing," the spinner is thrown upstream, slack is taken out of the line, followed by a slow retrieve. By feeling the "thump" of a blade, an expert will adjust the speed of the retrieve to gain maximum vibration. Watching the spinner through a drift, the angler will raise or drop the tip of the rod to lift the spinner above rocks and lower it into pockets.

Have you ever considered which direction the spinner is pointing when you throw it into the water? When I ask this question to anglers at my fishing seminar, the overwhelming answer is always, "hook downstream, blade upstream." Have you ever considered why summer steelhead frequently take a spinner sideways? Winter steelhead almost always take a spinner from the rear. Jed Davis wrote that he felt "side strikes" took place because his summer steelhead spinners lacked shank tubing on the hook. I have an alternate explanation.

When a spinner is thrown upstream, a large belly is immediately put into the line and quickly carries the spinner downstream. This belly acts like a sail and pulls the spinner with it. This means that the spinner is facing downstream, with the hook pointed upstream. If a steelhead were to take a spinner in this position, it would appear to be a "side strike." Most spinner experts attempt to quickly take as much belly out of the line as possible. Using a long rod to keep line off the water is helpful, but some belly is unavoidable. This is easy to see when fishing low, clear winter streams with fluorescent red tubing on a spinner.

In some cases, the belly of the line will eventually hit a "seam" of slow-moving water, causing the spinner to pass the belly of the line and begin to swing. When this happens, there is usually an increase in the speed the blade spins. Most of the time, the blade continues to spin pointing in a downstream direction until it catches up with the belly and the line straightens. As the spinner begins to "quarter" and move through the current, it is finally sitting in upstream position.

When fishing low on a drift, most strikes seem to occur as the spinner begins to cross the current. In this position, the spinner crosses directly in front of the steelhead and the fish sees the spinner from a rear view. For this reason, the bright fluorescent rear tape plays an important role.

In clear water, the steelhead will first see the spinner as it is facing downstream. The steelhead is able to see the spinner at maximum distance when the outside of the blade is colored a bright metallic silver or gold, or painted a "long-distance" color like blue, green, white, or yellow (depending on the water clarity). At moderate distances, the steelhead may see the spinner from the side and be able to see both the front and the rear of the spinning blade.

The higher on the drift that a steelhead holds, or the earlier in the cast that it strikes, the greater the importance of your front blade color. The lower on the drift or the later in the swing that the steelhead strikes, the greater the importance of the rear blade color.

This is an important consideration to make when discussing coloration of a spinner. Spinner color depends on your technique!

I met a spinner fisherman who swore by Panther Martin spinners. Within a few minutes of watching him fish, it became obvious why he did better with this type of spinner than he would with a French blade-type spinner. He positioned himself so that the spinner was seen from the front and sides by the fish. I suggest that you spend some time on a low, clear stream with a small piece of fluorescent tubing hooked to the end of your spinner. By doing this exercise a few times, you may get a better idea of when your spinner is facing upstream and when it faces downstream. I think you might be surprised.

Retrieves

In earlier chapters I discussed how I believe steelhead and salmon have directional vision. With salmon and kokanee, trolling spinners at eye level should be of bright fluorescent colors, but nickel or darker lures fished very deep are also very effective.

There are some specialty retrieving patterns that I will use when I switch color patterns. When fishing for winter steelhead with a silver and red spinner, I will typically retrieve at about 3/4 the depth of the water. When fishing summer steelhead with a light Summer Rain, I fish the spinner at about 1/2 depth. If I run a spinner through an area that I am sure holds fish and yet get no takers, I rest the water for a few minutes. My next pass through the area will come with a Summer Heat and/or Summer Deep.

When I fish the next time through, I attempt to "bottom bounce" the spinner and practically roll it along the bottom without retrieving. I adjust the drift by gently lifting the tip of the rod up when I hit bottom then drop it down until I hit again. This is a technique that Bill Herzog calls "Ringing the Dinner Bell," in his book *Spoon Fishing For Steelhead.*

This technique has been surprisingly effective with these darker patterns, further evidence of this directional vision in steelhead/salmon. This tactic will lose you some spinners, so I do not recommend it except in prime areas which you are sure contain fish.

There are two other specialty tactics that I try with spinners. During the summer, fish will often strike small dark spinners that are moving very slowly at the surface. Use a long rod and keep all of the line off the water. Try not to retrieve and hold the spinner high on the surface by adjusting your rod tip. The spinner should stay within a foot of the surface and "wake" the surface once in a while, but must move as slowly as possible. It's not an easy tactic, but it is very effective during some sunny summer days.

Another tactic that I borrowed from one of Bill Herzog's books is the "drift mend." I use this in deep, slow pools. I switch to an overweighted spinner and cast downstream. My first move is to draw the slack out of the line, then flip a mend upstream. I then lift the tip of the rod high and either hold the line with the bail open, or back reel. I feed out line and lower the tip of the rod to prevent the current from "pushing" the spinner off the bottom. This tactic results in a very slowly moving spinner with great line control as the spinner backs through a slow drift. This is the tactic that I have used to catch my two largest steelhead.

If you seriously want to spinner-fish for steelhead, try to master these three specialty tactics—bottom-bouncing, waking, and drift mending. There is a lot more to spinner-fishing than just casting and retrieving. Use your knowledge of "See Best" filters and backgrounds to make small adjustments in the color of your spinner before using these tactics.

Trolling Spinners

Large rainbow-colored spinners have become popular for fishing salmon and steelhead in large rivers, bays, and tidewater. Using the "See Best" System, there are eight basic underwater patterns. In moderate water temperatures, the long-distance color shifts are most important to consider.

General Principles

1. Brightest long-distance colors in clear water are white and fluorescent blue.
2. Brightest long-distance colors in blue water are fluorescent blue and fluorescent green.
3. Brightest long-distance colors in green water are fluorescent green and fluorescent yellow.
4. Brightest short-distance colors are fluorescent red and fluorescent orange.
5. Fluorescent red is of limited value at long range.
6. Use short-distance brightness colors close to the shaft of the spinner.
7. Use long-distance brightness colors farther from the center of rotation of the spinner. Using the opposite will make your blade look smaller.

Jed Davis' Book On Spinners

I agree with 95% of what I read in Jed Davis' book, *Spinner Fishing For Steelhead, Salmon, and Trout*. It remains "the bible" for steelhead spinner-fishermen. There are a few points where I disagree with Jed concerning his evaluation of color, particularly in "brand name spinners." In his book (pages 55-57), Davis outlines his opinions on some winter steelhead spinners. Some quotations include:

"Nickel...gives off an almost black finish."

"I'd prefer...nickel blade and body...to silver blade and fluorescent body."

"Bud's spinner...quality shank tubing."

"Metric spinner...tubing gives a faded appearance."

"Vibrax....no tubing on shank, extremely underweight...disqualify it as a steelhead spinner."

I disagree with some of these comments because they were made on the basis of visibility in air not under water. In underwater photography at over 100 feet in depth, it has been proven that nickel blades do not turn black under water. In deep blue water, nickel blades appear to turn blue. In deep, green water, nickel blades will appear to turn green.

Nickel blades are not as bright as silver blades under water, but they do not turn black.

The shank tubing on Bud's and Metric spinners are bright red and similar in material. Both tubings look bright in air and both will turn black in deep, green water. I consider both to be better for clear-water summer conditions. I would not call the shank tubing on a Metric spinner "faded" in appearance. The "quality" of the tubing on both spinners is excellent, but the color is poor.

The Vibrax Blue Fox spinner sinks very well and I would not consider it "underweight" for steelhead fishing. The fluorescent orange body is very bright under water. You cannot "disqualify" the Vibrax as a steelhead spinner when it is the most popular steelhead spinner in the Pacific Northwest.

Possibly in reference to this spinner, Jed stated that he would rather have an all-nickel spinner than a spinner with a silver blade and fluorescent painted body. From the standpoint of underwater visibility, a spinner with a silver blade and fluorescent painted body would be better than one that is all nickel.

Jed also wrote, "Technique is more important...give a beginner silver-plated spinners...and an expert tarnished brass...and the expert will outfish the beginner 3:1." What he meant was that even if a beginner had the greatest spinners in the world and an expert had the worst...the expert's skill would still allow him to outfish the beginner 3:1. This is a good point, but a bad example—tarnished brass can be an excellent finish for winter steelhead.

In January of 1997, my small, summer, tarnished brass spinners outfished my large, winter, silver-plated spinners 3:1. It was a high-water month, with the water being close to 40 degrees and milky green most of the month. All indications were that large #5 silver spinners should be effective, just as they had been a year earlier. So, why the difference?

In 1996, cold weather and ice kept many people off this stretch of the river. In 1997, there was more rain, but also more fishing pressure. I felt that the fish were "spooked" because of the amount of "eye-level" presentations that they had received from bright bait, jigs, and drift bobbers. I usually will not use the technique of "bottom-bouncing" a spinner during high-water months since it results in a huge number of snags. Since I knew fish were present, I decided to try this technique.

The most productive lure that I have used bottom-bouncing a spinner is the #2 Summer Heat. In Chapter 7 I discussed that many types of fish have color vision at eye-level, but better "dark on dark" contrast vision below eye-level. I used a small #2 black and tarnished brass spinner with heavy 12-pound-test line, rolled along the bottom.

I have tried "bottom-bouncing" large silver spinners and they are not as effective with this technique. Jed Davis' statement that an expert with "bad spinners" could outfish a beginner with "great spinners" was a poor example. I find that these small tarnished brass spinners are much better than large silver spinners...even in the winter time, when using this particular technique.

In Order To Be Fair To Jed...

He came up with a number of very valid conclusions about spinner color combinations. I am going to do a brief analysis of the underwater visibility of some of his favorite spinner patterns as listed on pages 93-95 in the third edition of his book. These spinners were constructed of Pen Tac components, tubing, and tape. The conclusions stated do not apply if the materials from other companies are used.

Winter Steelhead Standard: This spinner is usually made in a #5 with a Pen Tac silver-plated body and blade, fire orange tape on the rear of the blade, and matching tubing on the hook. The fire orange tape and tubing is very visible at short distance in green water of a low temperature. The Pen Tac silver finish is very bright at moderate distances in similar water conditions. An excellent winter steelhead spinner for water under 45 degrees!

Green Standard: This is the same silver spinner with Kelly green tape and tubing. The green tape and tubing are less bright at close range and brighter (than fire orange) at long distance. This makes a spinner that is more effective at moderate water temperatures. In a river like the Deschutes, with summer water temperatures and winter-type water clarity, this spinner should be highly visible. Since steelhead that are spawning immature also have eyes which are better able to see green objects, this should be a great combination for this location.

Columbia Gorge: This spinner consists of a 14K gold blade, with a black oxide body in size 5. The combination of 14K gold and black oxide body is more visible than other color combinations in stained water with moderate sunlight. Earlier in this chapter, I referred to this spinner design as a "black car with yellow fog lamps." This is a good combination to use when the water is really "foggy."

Summer Green: The Summer Green uses a #3 Pen Tac brass body and blade with Kelly green tape and tubing. This is a very visible spinner for a cloudy day, with water temperatures in the mid-50s. On a rainy summer day, summer steelhead would be expected to move out of the "chop" and into deeper tailouts. The warm temperatures make them reactive to lures that can be seen at long distance. It is essential that these lure colors not shift when they move closer. In this situation, the visual underwater background would be dark. The brass finish and green tape and tubing give excellent long-distance visibility, and remain constant as the fish moves closer. An excellent multi-use summer spinner for summer steelhead, coho, spring chinook, and trout! My experience has been that this type of spinner gets a greater percentage of very soft takes than other steelhead spinners. You must be very aware of "tip vibration" with this spinner and be prepared to set the hook whenever the vibrations stop.

McKenzie Dark: This was Jed's favorite summer steelhead spinner. It was made with a #2 black oxide Pen Tac blade and a #3 lightly tarnished brass body. When the water temperatures move into the high 50s, with direct sunlight, the summer steelhead move into the riffles and pocket water. Against a background of bright sun and white bubbles, this highly tarnished brass and black spinner is one of the most visible that you can use. It is one of the best designs for summer steelhead in full sunlight! The McKenzie Dark tends to attract thunderous hard strikes, often making it unimportant to "set the hook." Fish will move a long distance, either upward or downward to take this lure, then return to their holding position. When I fished this type of spinner, I would use a very slow action 10-foot noodle rod to absorb the impact of the first hit.

Ed's Pregnant: This spinner was described as a multi-use spinner consisting of a black oxide body and silver-plated blade, with black tape on the inside of the blade. I consider it a spinner that has good visibility in a wide range of conditions. In terms of long-distance visibility, a black body and silver blade spinner is much more visible than a silver body spinner with a black blade.

Through "trial and error," Jed Davis came to several conclusions that are confirmed using the "See Best" System. Silverplate is most effective in low light, moderately cloudy water, and low temperatures. Gold plate is most effective at higher lighting levels and muddier water. Black is most visible in very muddy water and in very clear water, in direct sun. Green is most visible in clear water, on a cloudy day. Fluorescent red and fluorescent orange are most effective in very cold water of moderate turbidity.

It is impressive to see how good a job Jed Davis did of selecting (through trial and error) components that were visible under water.

Other Spinner Component Companies

There were a number of other companies that sold spinner components for many years. Since Jed Davis sold his company, several new ones have started and are heavily advertising. Some of them are good and some are not.

I have used the Jed Davis 24K gold spinner blade very effectively. These blades were a very "yellow" gold. I recently bought "24K gold" spinner blades or spoons from five different component companies. In every case, these "24K gold" blades looked almost exactly like polished brass. When I tested these blades with my "See Best" filters, I could not tell the difference between these blades and those which were polished brass.

I purchased "24K gold" blades from several other companies and found only one other spinner that had the "yellow gold" appearance of the Jed Davis spinner. This was a #4 bass spinner from Mepps called a "WeedMaster." One spinner company that has been advertising "superior metal finishes" really bothered me. I purchased a set of 24K gold blades from them that looked like polished brass. I used the spinners three times in January and put them in storage. When I looked at the spinners again in June, the 24K gold finish had begun to develop spots of brown tarnish!

This company claimed that they used only "the best" metal finishes and that chrome and nickel were never used in the manufacturing of their spinner blades. Since this "24K gold" spinner developed brown tarnish, I decided to see what was actually under the plating. I put the spinner in a hydrogen peroxide bath and removed the "gold" finish. What I found was a chrome-plated blade!

Gold plating should not be removed by a bath of peroxide unless the coating is too thin or made of a material that is not really gold. "Gold" should not turn brown. The presence of a chrome undercoating may explain why this "gold" finish appeared so light. The Jed Davis "gold" was plated directly over brass, which made their blades more "yellow." I do not know whether this was a case of false advertising, a gold plating that was too thin, or a poor base metal. I do know that this was a very poor product that sold for a premium price. Please consider this experience if you build spinners out of "24K gold."

If I was building spinners from component companies, I would not purchase "24K gold" blades unless they were "yellow gold," and looked significantly different from polished brass. A true "yellow gold" is a great color for dirty water. Except for the Mepps WeedMaster, the "gold" spinners from the other ten companies (that I tested) were no different than polished brass.

The Future

There is much that can be done to make spinners more visible and effective. Only one company offers spinners that I believe are reasonably well designed in terms of color. I hope that the next few years will result in a breakthrough as companies begin to use the concepts that I am describing in this book.

Spinners can be made more visible under water using changes in color and body design. Most spinners and component companies sell spinner bodies which are straight cylinders. This is an inexpensive and adequate method of adding weight to the spinner, provided the spinners are made in the proper length. A few companies are making copies of the smooth double-tapered Jed Davis spinner body. There are some problems in the "double-tapered" design.

Contrary to what is advertised, spinner bodies are not "hydrodynamically designed." If they were, then every size of spinner body from a particular company would have the same proportions. When you go from a size 2, 3, 4, or 5 in any spinner company, the width of the spinner body does not change at the same rate as the length. "Double tapered" #5 spinner bodies are often short and stubby, while the #2s tend to be long and thin.

A better method is to develop one size and shape of spinner body that moves through the water with improved sinking/vibrational characteristics. This is done by placing models of the body in moving water and evaluating what changes in shape do to its movement patterns. Once the proper "angles" are determined, the sizes of the other bodies are determined by doing mathematical reductions.

The first spinner design of this type could hit the market as early as 1999. These will be spinners designed using underwater simulations and mathematical computations rather than "by guess and by golly." I expect that this "See Best" line of steelhead, salmon, and trout spinners will be built by Mepps/Sheldon's and available by Christmas of 1998. These spinners can be ordered by contacting the Clackamas River Trading Company or Mepps/Sheldon's.

I have designed eight spinners, using many of the principles described in this chapter. These spinners will be superior to anything on the market for the following reasons:

1. The correct color tubings.
2. The proper combination of color and color location.
3. A combination of extra-heavy and deep-cupped spinner blades.
4. A unique "sonic vibration" spinner body—a body that generates more underwater vibration than any on the market.
5. Special features like 24K gold-plated blades that actually look like gold, optically designed color patterns for maximum underwater visibility, and a special pattern cut into the brass body to directionally increase the distance at which it can be seen under water.

These spinners represent a huge technological jump in spinner design, and I believe that it will start a revolution in the fishing tackle industry. If you want a "first-hand" look at what the principles outlined in this book will do for the fishing tackle industry, call Kageyama's or Mepps and order a set. I've played with some prototypes of these designs and I think that they will be far superior to anything that you can currently buy (or build).

Kageyama's
P.O. Box 23744
San Jose, CA 95153-3744
1•800•361•3668

Mepps/Sheldon's
626 Center St., Dept. FG97
Antigo, WI 54409-2496
1•800•237•9877

Section V

Other Applications

CHAPTER 13

Applications: Steelhead Drift-Fishing

MANY FISHING AUTHORS LIKE BILL HERZOG AND JED DAVIS HAVE described a "framework" for lure selection based on water temperature, water clarity, and lighting conditions. The intent of this chapter is to demonstrate why their conclusions may be valid.

In Herzog's book *Color Guide to Steelhead Drift Fishing*, he advocates the use of large black and white spinning bobbers for muddy water. He suggests using large, bright fluorescent bobbers for low-visibility green water and moderate-sized pink drift bobbers for "classic steelhead green water." When fishing for summer steelhead under low and clear conditions, he describes his favorite rig as a small black Corkie with Boraxed eggs. In cold, clear winter conditions, he suggested small, bright fluorescent spinning bobbers. The value of these five lure color combinations can be demonstrated using five different "See Best" optical filter combinations.

1. For muddy drift conditions use a sandy background with one of the two muddy water filters.
2. For green water conditions use the brown background with the light or dark green water filters.
3. For warm summer conditions, use the light sand background with the long-distance blue filter.
4. For cold winter conditions, use the dark brown background with the short-distance blue filter.

Bill states that for fast-moving water conditions, "visual reaction strikes" take place and drift bobbers are as effective or more effective than bait. In slow-moving water, natural roe is considerably more effective than drift bobbers. The lures and color combinations that Bill suggests can be shown to be extremely visible in these water conditions using the "See Best" System.

"See Best" and Drift Bobbers

Drift bobbers are perhaps the only fishing lure type specifically designed for steelhead fishing. Drift bobbers come in many shapes and sizes and have only two common features—they float and they tend to be colored with fluorescent paints. Nearly all painted drift bobbers have fluorescent paints that hold their color well in deep green steelhead water. Whether you are using Corkies, Cheaters, Birdies, Spin-N-Glos, Pills, or other commercially made bobbers, they tend to be very consistent in their fluorescence.

When inspecting drift bobbers with the "See Best" filters you will notice four patterns:

1. There are some bobbers that are very bright in certain water conditions and very dark in others. These tend to be the bright, solid-color fluorescent orange, red, or pink bobbers.
2. The second type of bobber is one that uses combinations of colors, which results in less overall brightness but more versatility. Common examples of this are pink/pearl, rainbow, or green/orange.
3. The third type of bobber is one that results in a black and white appearance in a variety of water conditions. Any large bobber with sharply defined black lines is a possibility for a muddy-water lure.
4. The fourth type is by far the least common. These are dark lures painted with non-fluorescent or metallic finishes and which achieve a dark appearance under water with many water conditions.

It is easy to pick out bobbers that would be visible in various water conditions. The main question to consider is whether to use a "general" color that has some attraction under a wide range of conditions, or to use several "specialty" bobbers that are bright in only certain conditions. Most drift fishermen tend to go toward "general use" bobbers.

"See Best" and Roe Cures

Many "home-made" roe cures (even those with large amounts of red dye) turn out to be almost black in green water. The color of the eggs appears to be a result of oxidation and the use of non-fluorescent dyes. Older eggs appear to be much darker under water. Some of the newer fluorescent egg cures appear to be quite bright. There is considerable difference between Borax and sulfite cures that use fluorescent dyes. Borax cures tend to brighten the skeins in a "speckled" pattern, while sulfite cures tend to get into the egg itself. It is likely that natural roe will appear dark under most deep-water conditions.

Some authors have suggested that sulfite cures improve the color at the expense of taste—this possibility is outside the scope of this book. A problem with dyes in roe cures is that the color washes out quickly. Some cures retain their underwater brightness, even after 3 or 4 casts in the water. These you can discover by rinsing out samples of your eggs several times and then testing them.

Yarns

Yarns are very unpredictable and must be tested. Each piece of yarn must be tested to identify its actual underwater color, you cannot rely on the "See Best" optical filter lists. Many pink yarns will turn orange in green water and purple in clear water.

Beads

Beads may be a useful addition. My personal preference is to use "economy" beads of "lower quality." The shiny surfaces with bubbles, cracks, and imperfections reflect light and may make the bead more visible than the high-quality matte-finish beads without imperfections. I usually use fluorescent plastic beads for drift-fishing green water. Red glass beads appear to turn black in green water. I have read many advertisements that claim "high-quality glass beads hold their color under water." I disagree with this statement. Under most water conditions, fluorescent plastic beads are brighter than glass beads under water.

"High-quality" ground beads are more durable than injection-molded plastic beads, and this may be an issue when using these beads to make lures that you expect to use for several fishing trips.

Glass beads are more visible than plastic in some clear-water conditions. This is because glass that is the same color as the water will tend to "sparkle" more than plastic because of the light-bending properties of the material. Red glass beads may be very effective in clear water when a dark lure is desirable. Red glass beads can be effective in summer fishing for trout and in clear-water conditions for salmon or steelhead. Realize that you are actually fishing a dark, gray-red bead under water.

I read an article about "bobber and bait" fishing that stated clear glass beads used as weights would be invisible under water. This is not true. Clear glass sparkles under water and is certainly not "invisible." If you wish to use glass beads as weights, they will have less visibility on dark, cloudy days. On sunny days, consider using glass beads that have a matte finish.

Orange beads (plastic or glass) appear to hold some color in all clear and green water conditions and are more visible than red at long distance. Yellow and green beads have some use in clearer water conditions. Some experts claim that the only colors that a drift-fisherman needs are pink, white, and black. Other people say that all you need is pink and white. To some extent, both are correct.

Colors used in drift fishing can be broken up into three groups: bright, light, and dark. "Bright" colors include: red, fire, orange, and pink (all fluorescent). "Light" colors include: white, yellow, green, gold, chrome, and silver. "Dark" colors include: prism, metallic, blue, dark green, brown, non-fluorescent red/orange, and black.

To some extent, all you need might be one color from each group and the suggestion of pink, white, and black seems to follow that rule. The quality of the color is more important than the color itself. It is important that the underwater fluorescence of the color be as bright and true as possible. There is a wide variation between the brightness or fluorescence of different materials. Blue, purple, non-fluorescent red/orange, and prisms may be "bright" in some water conditions and "dark" in others.

Many "fluorescent" reds and pinks take on an orange hue under many water conditions. This is why different colors may be effective in the same water conditions. Two colors that look different in air may look the same under water. I urge you to stop thinking in terms of a "best color." It is the "quality" of the color, rather than the color itself that makes it effective or visible. All fluorescent reds are not created equal. When you work with only the highest-quality paints and dyes, very few colors are needed. Drift bobbers simplify the color selection process because every pink drift bobber that I have tested appears bright in clear or green water.

Basic Considerations Of Color And drift Fishing

Drift fishing involves the use of a bait or lure, connected by a leader to a relatively heavy weight which keeps the bait in close proximity to the bottom of a river. This technique is often used in water of limited visibility, when fishing for salmon and steelhead.

Lure colors should give the best contrast in deep water at short distance. With drift-fishing, it is considered unlikely that a fish will move long-distance to investigate a lure that is far away. The exception to this is when a fish is slow to react to a lure that has passed nearby, and is forced to pursue it downstream. In this situation, a fish may appear to be moving a long distance to take your lure, when it is actually relatively close to it during most of the process. The key words to remember are "short distance, deep water, and contrast."

Under most conditions, drift-fishermen will use "combination" lures, a drift bobber with yarn and possibly bait. This results in most lures being at least three different colors. The successful lure patterns of most drift-fishermen tend to include one color of maximum short-range brightness and a color of intermediate-range brightness.

Bait has the advantage of scent and taste—being most effective in water that is slow-moving. Color has its greatest use in water that is very fast-moving. The disadvantage of bait is color. Even bait which has been dyed will not retain its brightness for long periods of time under water (with the exception of "silver" baits like cut herring). The faster and heavier the water flow, the more quickly the fluorescent dyes (and underwater visibility) will be rinsed out of the bait.

Using a drift bobber allows an angler to have bright and predictable color on his drift lure. Drift bobbers also increase the visibility of your lure by floating and suspending it above the river bottom.

Some conclusions reached by many drift-fishermen include:

Bright red fluorescent drift bobbers are most effective when the water is very cold, the steelhead are holding deeper than average, or when the rivers are muddy. They are most effective when either the fish cannot see long-distance things, or are unwilling to move on a lure that has been presented at a distance.

Fluorescent pink, orange, and white drift bobbers are most effective under "classic" winter steelheading conditions. They are most effective when fish are able to see the lures at moderate distance, or are prepared to move moderate distances to take a lure.

Yellow and green lures are effective in warmer conditions when there is improved water clarity. They are valuable when the fish are at their maximum activity level and will move long distance to take a lure.

Black is effective when visibility in the water presents a bright background either because of poor water clarity or a very bright sun. It is also effective when warmer water temperatures encourage fish to rise to the surface to take lures.

Drift bobbers have the most consistent underwater visibility of any lure used by steelheaders. If a fisherman were to limit himself to a small number of variables, it would be pink, white, and black. The most common underwater appearance of drift-fishing rigs are combinations of these three colors. An example of this would be a pink and white drift bobber, pink yarn, and Boraxed eggs. The natural-colored eggs would take on the appearance of black under water.

Since the quality of color in drift bobbers tends to be excellent, the main color concern for drift-fishermen is the bait, and to a lesser extent, the yarn.

From an underwater visibility standpoint, the weakness of drift-fishing is the difficulty in keeping fluorescent red color on bait (it rinses off), and the inability to have true bright, reflective silver. The advantage of drift fishing is the ability to get the lure close enough to the fish that it is easily seen.

I have one friend who fishes with a pink/pearl Corkie, white yarn, and eggs all the time. I have another friend that fishes totally with a rainbow Birdie and sand shrimp. Both fishermen have their bases covered most of the time.

CHAPTER 14

Feathers And Fur Fly Fishing

A STORE MANAGER SAYS, "I'VE SOLD 'MACK'S CANYONS' FOR MANY years. I thought they were all the same, but when I put them under the "See Best" Filter some of them look like a Mack's Canyon and others just look black and white!"

Point #1: It is hard to get true bright fluorescent colors in feathers and fur.

Point #2: Different parts of feathers and fur take up dyes differently so there is a quality-control issue.

Point #3: With feathers and fur, there are many different types of "white." Small amounts of blue, yellow, or pink undertones can make certain whites much more (or less) visible under water in some conditions.

Quality Control: More than any other type of fishing method, the fly fisherman has problems with quality control. I urge you to examine large numbers of flies of "the same" pattern with the "See Best" deep, green water filter. You may be surprised to see that flies that you think are the same, may look very different from each other under water.

Picture 14-1 (on page 151) shows a large selection of fly-tying materials which were purchased at a nationally known fly fishing shop. The materials appear to be bright purple, blue, orange, or red in room lighting. Picture 14-2 shows the same materials under the "See Best" green water filter. The orange hackle in the upper left-hand corner is the only sample that stays bright. All the other materials turn black, including another piece of orange hackle. Steelhead flies tied with these materials would turn dark when fished under water.

The brightest fly materials are yarns, but even these are not as bright as fluorescent beads and paints. Yarn flies do not have the action of fur or feathers, although they are effective in some conditions. Tinsel is not as bright as silver-plated metal lures since it is thin and almost translucent, showing off light of the underlying material.

Factors such as dye lots, bleaching of materials by water, and the time/temperature of the dying process can cause changes in underwater visibility of materials even though they appear to be similar in air.

Pictures 14-3 and 14-4 show ten flies in room lighting and with the "See Best" Green Water Filter. Seven of these flies appear to turn dark. It is likely that all seven of these flies would be more effective if they were tied with materials that stayed bright under water.

Steelhead Flies

From the standpoint of underwater color there are four basic color types used in effective steelhead flies.

1. Flies tied with fluorescent materials or which have large "eyes" painted with fluorescent detail.
2. Flies tied with large amounts of bright non-fluorescent or mildly fluorescent fur in red, pink, or orange. These flies appear to be bright but actually behave more like black and white flies under water.
3. Black flies, with small amounts of white or other colors. Many fly fishermen consider black to be their best summer steelhead color. Black flies are most visible under bright, clear conditions where the fish are either viewing the fly against surface reflection or through white air bubbles in chop or pocket water.
4. Flies designed for ocean or clear water conditions which are based on green/blue, silver, and white.

Steelhead in Rivers

"Any color fly will work for steelhead, as long as it is black." This is a statement I read many years ago in a fly fishing magazine. Many fly fishermen may still agree with it. By looking at materials, fishing tactics, and steelhead behavior, it becomes clear how such an opinion develops.

Many steelhead fly fishermen prefer to work in warmer, clear water conditions. Under these conditions, a steelhead is more likely to rise and strike a fly presented above it. From below, the steelhead views the fly against the bright surface film, therefore a dark black fly will give maximum contrast. The surface film is multi-colored: combining black with a few non-fluorescent colors may give the fly visibility under a range of lighting conditions.

I've tested many beautiful multi-colored steelhead flies under the "See Best" Deep Green Water Filter and found that many of them just looked "black and white." A very small number of flies will appear mildly fluorescent. Even these materials tend not to be as bright as similar dyes applied to metal or plastic lures. Fluorescent dyes applied to feathers and fur are absorbed irregularly and it is common to see the fluorescent aspects of the dyes absorbed only into part of the material.

If you examined a strip of fluorescent red rabbit fur with the "See Best" Deep, Green Water Filter, you would probably note that the skin appears black, while parts of the fur may appear brighter than others. Different parts of a feather take up the fluorescent dyes in different ways. Parts of a "red" feather may appear red, black, or white when viewed with the long-distance filter. Dubbing materials may also be unpredictable in their underwater appearance.

These types of problems, plus the difficulty in reaching the bottom during heavy river flows, make fly fishing for steelhead very difficult in winter.

There are some steelhead flies which use fluorescent yarn: such as Glo-Bugs, but these are still not as bright as drift bobbers (Pictures 14-5 and 14-6). Their disadvantage is that they give less "action" in the water than other materials. Pink and orange are the easiest fluorescent colors to achieve when working with fur and feathers. Carefully test all flies tied in these colors as there is considerable variation in underwater visibility of different materials.

Certain types of "white" hair or fur will reflect underwater light in an interesting manner, resulting in high contrast. This opens up a new area for color testing with the "See Best" filters. Other steelhead fishing materials use solid colors with limited texture. Furs or hair (such as moose or natural buck-tail) offer multi-colored strands with variations of white, which react in different ways to the filtered underwater light and can result in increased contrast. Some materials are exceptionally bright in clear water conditions. It is important to remember that there are many different types of white. Small amounts of blue, yellow, or pink undertones can make certain types of white on feathers or fur much more (or less) visible under water in some conditions.

For green or muddy water look for products which have some degree of fluorescence. Carefully check all dyed materials for fluorescence. These types of flies will offer greater visibility in green water. The deeper that you run your flies, the more important the deep-water color shift becomes. Like all steelhead lures, increased visibility can also be achieved through increased size.

The deep-water color shifts can affect wet flies and streamers. Purple can be a valuable color in clear water. Purple will turn black in green water, but may remain very bright in clear or blue water.

Dry Flies

The deep-water color shift is not important when fishing on the surface. If you intend to fish dry flies in clear water, test them using the blue long-distance filter.

General-purpose flies are black/white, but the goal of the white is to provide contrast for the black. Look for flies with whites that are not uniform in color and colors which remain visible from long distance.

Salt Water

In very clear water or ocean conditions consider flies which are blue/green, silver, white, or metallic. Metallic fly-fishing materials are not as reflective under water as metal lures such as spinners and spoons. Test the visibility of your saltwater flies using either the deep water blue or the long-distance blue filters. An important adjustment to make in saltwater fishing is that underwater conditions tend to be a little more blue/gray in sea water, while they are a little more blue/brown in clear rivers. This is probably due to ocean water containing a larger amount of sand or inorganic suspended dust particles, while rivers contain more decaying plant material. It is important to remember that even though both the ocean and rivers appear green on the surface, it is more likely that the ocean is blue under the surface.

Check shallow-running flies in the ocean using the long-distance blue filter. Bright fluorescent or metallic blues/greens, whites, and silvers tend to give you the best long-distance visibility under these conditions. For deeper-running flies, test using the deep-water blue filter. These same colors, along with a few bright fluorescent accents, will give you optimum visibility under these conditions.

"Matching The Hatch"

Color matching potential food sources is a cornerstone of fly fishing for all fish except salmon and steelhead (which do not tend to feed in fresh water). Food sources tend to be low visibility. Aquatic insects, fish, or animals that live on river bottoms are drab brown, green, or black. Size, profile, and color all contribute to a fly which matches potential food sources.

I suggest that you consider examining a variety of aquatic insects and your fly materials with the "See Best" deep-water blue filter and the blue long-distance filter. What you will discover from this exercise is that it is possible to color match an insect to a fly (in room lighting) and have them appear very different under water. Different dyes will shift color under water in different ways. Pay special attention to how different types of "white" fur or feathers behave with the "See Best" blue and green filter/flashlights.

One of my favorite spinners for summer steelhead is a green and gold #3 spinner that is about 1 1/4 inch long. I was fishing the Upper Clackamas with a friend who hadn't been very successful in the past when fishing for steelhead. I was fishing a green and gold spinner that had a piece of green shank tubing. My friend was fishing a spinner without tubing or a spinner with a piece of almost clear tubing. His spinner appeared to be slightly less than an inch in length. Over a period of less than two hours, he hooked and landed a pair of beautiful nine-pound summer steelhead. This was the first time that he had ever caught two steelhead in a day—and a day I got "skunked" fishing the same water.

I was fishing the same water but the steelhead were apparently keying off a slightly shorter lure. Returning to the same river the following week, I hooked steelhead using spinners with the shank tubing removed. I cannot explain why the steelhead were selective. It was interesting to note that they refused to hit long lures with size 2 and 3 blades, but they would hit either a 2 or a 3 spinner as long as the tubing had been removed.

I have seen the same phenomena fishing for many different types of fish. I have seen times where the fish seem to strike only size 0 spinners or single eggs, avoiding larger offerings. I've had numerous trips trout fishing in lakes where fish only seemed to strike tiny balls of Powerbait™ that were barely large enough to cover a size 16 hook. In some cases, a quarter inch in length may be all the difference needed to elicit a strike.

This does not mean that it is always better to go small. I have seen fishermen "limit-out" fishing golf ball-sized balls of roe, huge 6 spinners, or giant plugs, while other equally skilled fishermen using smaller baits went home empty. When "matching the hatch" or finding the most effective lure, you must consider size, profile, and contrast.

Three Fly Fishing Myths

1. Using fluorescent fishing line to tie ribbing in a fly incorporates ultraviolet into a tie.
Fluorescent fishing line does not give off ultraviolet light. Fluorescent colors convert light of short wavelength (like ultraviolet, blue, or green) and give off other visible colors. They do not require ultraviolet and they do not emit off ultraviolet. A fluorescent red lure which is struck with blue light will emit red light. Using fluorescent fishing line will give the fly increased brightness at longer distance and greater depths, but this will not be caused by "ultraviolet reflection."

2. Fish think that Glo-Bugs are eggs of a mountain whitefish.
I read an article in which Glo-Bugs were used to catch trout in California. In the article it said that when 1 mm gold whitefish eggs were present, fly fishermen used 8-10 mm Glo-Bugs in pink or red. This makes no sense at all. A trout is not going to think that a bright 10 mm red puff of yarn is actually a tiny 1 mm clear, golden fish egg!

I would propose a few other possibilities. One reason that Glo-Bugs are round could be that their compact shape may give a better underwater drift. These yarn flies could also be effective because they are more visible than other types of flies in deep cloudy water. Drift fishermen catch fish using the same yarn without bothering to shape it into round balls.

It makes no sense to claim that you are "matching the hatch" with something the wrong color and ten times as big as the real thing.

3. "Black is the brightest, highest contrast color, under water."
Black is a popular and effective color for fly fishing. It is a high-contrast color, given the conditions and tactics that most fly fishermen use. If you are fishing on a sunny day, in clear water, and the fish is looking up at your lure on the surface, against the film, or in shallow water, black is a high-contrast color. It will hold its contrast in these conditions at both short and long distance. If the water is very muddy and the fish are shallow, black will be a high-contrast short-distance color.

There are many conditions where black is not as visible. Black is not highly visible in deep water, on dark days, at long distance, or in moderately cloudy water. Black is not highly visible below the line of sight on dark days or in dark water. Black is not a popular color with steelhead drift fishermen because of the differences in their fishing tactics, and because they have the benefit of brighter, more fluorescent materials.

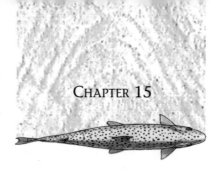

CHAPTER 15

Applications: Pulling Plugs

THERE ARE MORE COLORS, TEXTURES, AND FINISHES WITH PLUGS THAN any other lure used for steelhead or salmon fishing. Underwater color analysis on this type of lure has a huge number of variables. The primary "fish-catching" features for plugs are probably vibration, movement, and location. Because it is a very complicated lure, small differences in the placement of screws, hooks, and diving lips can cause huge differences in performance. "Tuning" a plug refers to making it track straight, but other differences can cause vertical or lateral action which may be positive or negative. Different plugs run at different depths and some plugs run better at slow water speeds. This information is important to know when selecting colors.

Although there are a large number of plug colors and combinations, the "See Best" filters will show that many of them look very similar under water. There are a few basic rules that should be considered.

1. Test all your plugs and carefully note what each one looks like under the "See Best" filters.

2. Pay special attention to the metallic colors, many metallic colors turn very dark. Use dark metallic in bright sun, bright metallic in medium sun, and colored fluorescents on dark days.

3. Use colored fluorescents on plugs that run very deep.

4. In clear to moderate clarity water, use blue plugs for blue water and green plugs for green water. In water with more "color," use more fluorescents, gold, or black and white.

5. Consider long-distance color shifts unless the water is very cold.

An interesting exercise would be to examine the plug colors recommended by Mike Laverty in his book *Plug Fishing For Steelhead*. Mike suggests painted plugs (which appear bright with the "See Best" Deep Green Water Filter) on cloudy days and metallic plugs (which appear dark) on sunny days.

In brown water he lists large Hot Shots in size 25/35 in glows/fluorescent, chartreuse/fire, and copper/blues. He includes Wiggle Warts in metallic blue/red speck, metallic, hot green specks, gold/fluorescent, red stripe, or black and white. Examine these with the two "See Best" muddy water filters.

In green water he lists medium Hot Shots in cop car, metallic pink, silver/blue, pirate silver/blue, these are lures that show good long-distance visibility with the "See Best" long-distance green filter.

In low clear water he lists small Hot Shots, in colors such as crawfish, shrimp, and copper, which turn dark with the "See Best" blue long-distance filter.

Fluorescent fire red is suggested for slow deep water. Test these with the deep-water green filter.

I encourage you to look through Mike's book and test several plugs from each group with the blue/green/brown long-distance filters and see how your observations agree with his recommendations.

Some More Advanced Tips From Mike

Because of the angle the plug rides relative to the fish you'll want to pay special attention to what a plug looks like from behind. Mike showed me a few of his custom plugs, which included a small fluorescent insert placed into the tail. Mike drills a small hole into the bottom rear of the plug and inserts a fluorescent foam orange or pink puff ball. This ball is covered with scent, which gives it additional fish-attracting properties. As a fish views the plug from the rear, it sees the bright bouncing ball contrasted against the belly of the plug.

I would suggest the possibility of using foam balls of fluorescent pink, chartreuse, or green to contrast against plugs with different belly colors. Selecting the color of the puff ball requires an understanding of whether the rest of the plug appears bright or dark under water. Metallic plugs appear very bright in air, but may have an appearance which is difficult to predict under water.

Several metallic orange plugs are very bright. These metallic orange plugs may range in brightness from pink/orange to almost yellow when viewed with the green water filter. Metallics with a pink cast may be more effective in the middle of winter when water temperatures and fish metabolism are very low. Metallic orange lures with a yellow cast may be more visible from long range and more effective for early or late winter fishing when the water temperature is higher and the fish are more willing to move longer distances to take the lure.

With plugs, I assume that the major "fish-attracting" features involve scent and vibration. If you have a plug with exceptional qualities in these areas, it will be productive in a wide range of conditions, including a few where it does not have exceptional visibility.

Buzz Ramsey has made many statements about the new Fire Tails by Luhr-Jensen. He says that most plugs were designed backwards, with the attractant colors being painted on the diving bill. This may lead to many fish either not seeing the color or attacking the front of the lure. Side strikes are common when plug fishing. He claims that this problem is eliminated by putting fluorescent paint on the tail, and doing this eliminates the need for a front hook in these plugs.

Mike Laverty customizes many of the plugs he uses for muddy water by drawing zigzags on the back with a black felt pen. Examine what that does to the visibility of a lure by using the two muddy water filters.

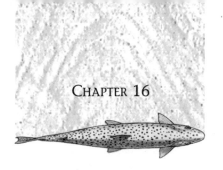

Chapter 16

Applications: Marabou Jigs For Steelhead

POINT #1: SOME "FLUORESCENT" RED OR ORANGE FEATHERS ARE OVER five times brighter than others under water.

Point #2: Most marabou jigs turn black in deep water and are best suited to shallow and clear water presentations.

Point #3: The most reliable way of getting fluorescent red on a jig is to paint the jig head, add fluorescent red beads, fluorescent red yarn, or fluorescent red thread.

"Bobber and jig" is one of the most popular methods for fishing steelhead in the Pacific Northwest. The strength of this method is the ease with which a fisherman can learn to present a lure at the proper location and speed. Nick Amato of *Salmon Trout Steelheader* Magazine has written that he considers it "the best" method for the beginner to catch steelhead. It is a tremendous technique for catching steelhead in clear shallow water. A strength (and a weakness) with this technique is that some marabou jigs turn dark in deep water.

Summer Steelhead

Bobber and jig experts seldom set their jigs deeper than 3 feet when fishing summer conditions. With shallow presentations, deep-water color shifts are not important. Long-distance color shifts can come into play.

Most marabou jigs used in summer steelhead fishing come in two colors. Most effective summer steelhead jigs contain either one or two colors which turn dark under water. Popular combinations include: black/red, red/black, orange/yellow, black/white, red/white, and purple/pink.

These jigs are a reasonable choice for shallow clear-water conditions. With shallow presentations (during summer), the fish are either looking up at a bright sky or looking up at a very bright surface film of white air bubbles. Dark looking jigs give high visibility. Consider testing these jigs using a long-distance blue filter and either a light blue background for early morning/evening, or a silver background for daylight conditions. Black gives maximum contrast early or late in the day, while moderately dark lures (like red or non-fluorescent orange) give sufficient contrast in sunlight. Jigs are most effective for summer steelhead early or late in the day.

Winter Steelhead Green Water

Cold water and limited visibility make bobber and jig fishing less predictable. Jim Bradbury recommends his orange/yellow, yellow, and chartreuse jigs for winter steelhead. Winter steelheading involves setting the jigs deeper and fishing them in water that has limited visibility. Under these conditions the jigs will be affected by deep-water color shifts.

In testing the Bradbury jigs, yellow and chartreuse exhibited the least amount of deep-water color shift. After testing his jigs with the deep, green water filter, I would agree that these are his three brightest deep-water colors. They are a reasonable choice for fishing green winter steelhead water.

There are some jigs of other colors from other companies that test out bright using the green water filter. The best "winter steelhead" jig in one company might be yellow, while another company might consider its best winter color to be red or pink. The differences lie in the dyes used in their marabou. There is some difficulty in finding good bright fluorescent red or fluorescent pink marabou. Other methods of adding fluorescence to these jigs include adding fluorescent beads, yarn, or paint on the jig head. Test various designs of jigs with the deep, green water filter.

Specialty Colors

There are a few situations where specialty colors like purple which be effective in certain conditions. In Chapter 7 of this book, I describe how the color vision of salmon and steelhead changes when they become spawning ripe. Spawning immature fish are readily able to see short wavelength colors like purple/blue. Spawning mature fish are better able to see long wavelength colors like orange/pink/red. When you test the purple jigs with the various underwater filters, there is only one condition where it has high visibility—clear water. In Oregon, the only time that you are likely to encounter spawning immature fish in very clear water is in the spring. Purple jigs or flies are very effective in some sections of the Clackamas River during clear-water conditions when fishing for chinook in the spring.

Multi-season

The red jigs of some companies are non-fluorescent and turn dark when viewed in deep water from long distance. These jigs tend to be best suited for fishing shallow in water where the fish do not view the lure from a long distance. There are two situations where this could take place.

The long-distance vision of a fish will be limited if it is holding in pocket water, behind rocks, or in water that has a broken surface with a lot of suspended air bubbles. These are common occurrences that are searched out by jig fishermen pursuing summer steelhead. If the water is very cold and clear, the fish will tend to disregard the lure at long distance. This is a second situation where a non-fluorescent red jig may be effective.

The non-fluorescent red jig can be considered a "multi-season" jig since it is visible in one summer and one winter water condition. It is important to note that this color is poorly visible in classic dark winter steelhead green water.

Other Observations

A weakness in marabou jig materials is that "fluorescent" dyes are not as bright in deep water as the materials used in other fishing methods. Another weakness is that some of the dyes are taken into the feathers in a consistent manner, while others are taken up unevenly. A black jig might appear all black and require some additional red/orange/white materials to set it off and give contrast. Many other colors may also take up in an uneven manner with part of the feather appearing colored while other parts remain white. This may be an advantage and it is something I look for when selecting winter steelhead jigs.

The fine fibers of some marabou may stay white so some pink marabou jigs appear pink/white in deep water, while others appear a flat pink, dull orange, or dull purple. The goal in selecting (or constructing) marabou jigs is similar to the goal in tying flies—you want to give visibility with movement, and the illusion of depth. With flies this is achieved using multiple types of hackle, thread, and fur. With marabou jigs this is done by properly selecting marabou and adding other materials such as paint, thread, yarn, or beads.

Conclusions

Jigs that turn dark in green and blue water may be good choices for fishing summer steelhead. Jigs which retain some deep-water brightness are best for winter steelhead fishing. Fluorescent yellow tends to be one of the brightest marabou colors in deep water. There are very few bright fluorescent red marabou feathers presently on the market. The easiest way to add underwater brightness to a winter steelhead jig is through the addition of fluorescent painted jig heads, fluorescent red/orange beads, or fluorescent red yarn.

The weakness of many marabou jigs is their color. Their strength is in their movement. Do not do anything to a marabou jig that will restrict its ability to move in the water. Marabou jigs remain one of the most effective methods for catching steelhead. By understanding the weakness of the material, you can begin to understand why the most effective colors for marabou jigs differ from the most effective colors for other types of lures.

Section VI

Other Fish, Other Methods, And Other Senses

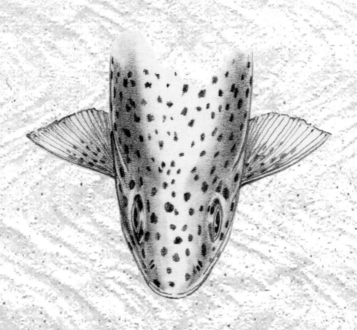

CHAPTER 17

"Hot Local Tips"
For Other Types Of Fishing

COHO, CHUMS, BLACKMOUTH, BLUEGILLS, MUSKIE, SALT WATER
What do they have in common?

Green Wool In White Water (Canada)

Fresh chrome coho will often hold high in a pool, just under the white water. They gather energy for their run up the next series of rapids, then rest high in the next pool. The more spawning-mature dark fish move less and hold in the lower tailouts and deep central areas of a pool. The rolling fish seen in the middle of deep pools are almost always dark fish.

Dark fish tend to have eyes that are most sensitive to the light of longer wavelength reds and orange. Fresh, spawning immature fish are more likely to still have eyes that are green sensitive. In clear blue and light green water, fluorescent greens and yellows can be seen from the greatest distance.

If a coho salmon is holding in white water and looks upstream, objects will be moving past it quickly. If a fluorescent red lure was presented in front of it, the lure would appear dark and difficult to see at a distance. As the lure moved close to the fish, the lure would rapidly brighten. The fish would have a few brief moments to determine whether or not to take the red lure.

If a fluorescent green yarn lure was thrown in front of the same coho, it would appear bright and visible from a greater distance. First because green light travels further in blue and green water. Second because the eyes of a fresh coho that is holding in white water are more adapted to seeing green objects. The coho would be aware of the lure when it is further away and have additional time to determine whether or not to take the lure. Both of these factors result in more fish being hooked.

In general terms, fishing with red lures low on the drift will increase your chances of catching dark fish. Fishing green lures high on a drift (under the white water) will increase your chances of catching bright fish. There will be some exceptions, but these are general patterns.

Green Food Coloring In Herring (Puget Sound)

I know of several Washington fishermen who dye their herring with green food coloring before fishing for blackmouth salmon in Puget Sound. This tactic goes along with the next tactic I will describe which is "Blue Bleach Herring." Why do fishermen dye herring green in Washington and blue in Oregon? Why do they dye the herring at all?

If you closely examine fish scales under bright light, you will see that what initially looks like a silver reflection, actually consists of a number of different colors. The color of the light reflected off fish scales varies depending on the angle that light is reflected. The color of reflection could look silver, with red, pink, yellow, green, or blue undertones. If you examine these fish scales through one of the "See Best" System Blue or Green Water Filters, the red and pink undertones appear to turn gray. In blue water, the yellow undertones will also darken. In green water, the yellow undertones will stay bright.

When you take a herring and dye it green, the ability of the fish scales to reflect the green, yellow, and blue increases. This green dye eliminates the red and pink undertones and converts to light green. When this green herring is placed in green water (in Puget Sound), it appears significantly brighter in deep water than undyed herring. Natural herring would appear silver/green with gray undertones (the pink). Green-dyed herring would appear a brighter silver/green without any gray. Increased brightness means increased contrast in deep water.

Blue Bleach Herring (Oregon Coast)

In the ocean, as opposed to tidewater, there is probably less suspended decaying plant material in the water, so there is probably a greater tendency for blue light to penetrate. In these conditions, the yellow undertones of fish scales would also darken in deep water. Using a blue bleach will get rid of most of the yellow, pink, and red undertones of the fish scales and result in a similar increase in brightness/contrast for cut herring in a different water condition.

Green Yarn For Chums (Oregon and Washington)

A salmon coming out of the ocean would be expected to have "saltwater eyes"—best able to see objects which are light green. On clear ocean beaches and the clear lower stretches of rivers where chums spawn, these light green lures can be seen from further away. In the deep green oceans from which the chums recently came, all of the food sources appear in shades of green.

Once they are on the spawning beds, they may start to see pink eggs from chums that have spawned earlier. I suspect that if you fished chums heavily, there would be an increasing tendency of late-arriving chums to strike pink lures. For chums that have not reached the spawning beds, green should be the best color.

Metallic Green And Metallic Blue (California Coast)

In the clear blue waters off the Southern California coast, blues and greens carry far greater distances than other colors. On sunny days, the flash of a metallic lure is far brighter than on cloudy days. In warm water, the higher metabolism of the fish will cause it to move further to take a lure. All three of these factors combine to make metallic greens and blues a powerful combination when fishing on sunny days in clear blue oceans.

Red Thread On Jigs For Bluegills (Almost Everywhere)

Bluegills live in warm shallow water with large amounts of decaying plant material. These waters tend to transmit a larger amount of red light. Bluegills do not travel a long distance to strike a lure since they are small and territorial. They tend to hold in areas with a lot of brush and cover, so they will not become aware of a lure until it is close. These factors make it an advantage to add non-fluorescent red thread to jigs used for fishing bluegills.

Spinner Fishing For Muskies In Stained Water (Midwest)

Muskies are a warm-water fish, with peak activity in water over 70 degrees. A popular method of fishing in June or July is the fast retrieve of a French bladed spinner with a bucktail. In stained water, popular colors are fire tiger blade and tail, chartreuse blade with black/chartreuse tail, fluorescent orange blade with black/chartreuse tail, or a gold blade with a black bucktail.

Much has been written about the need for Muskie lures to match local forage fish, but it is interesting to compare the underwater visibility of these lures to steelhead lures which would be used in similar water clarity. The main difference between the musky and steelhead water is that muskies are in lakes and the "stained" water is 20 to 30 degrees warmer. The main difference with the musky spinner is that it has a bucktail, rather than rubber tubing. The bucktail is very difficult to dye properly in bright orange and red colors.

In stained water, top steelhead spinners are:
1. Gold and Black (or Chartreuse and Black)
2. Gold and Fluorescent Red

When examining a popular fire tiger muskie spinner with the "See Best" System stained water filters, I see that the blade appears bright yellow/black and the tail appears black, with a touch of yellow.

The other three popular spinners follow the pattern of yellow (or gold) and black. The main difference is that at low water temperatures, steelhead will not move long distances to strike a lure and only see the rear of a slow-moving lure before striking. For that reason, the attractor colors must be placed on the rear of the spinner. The musky will get a side view of a spinner moving by rapidly. It is important that the color be apparent from a wide side profile. Taking into consideration the weakness of bucktail or squirrel tail as a material holding fluorescent colors, these color patterns make sense. The only practical place for putting fluorescent red coloring is on the outside of the French blade. Popular stained water musky spinners are basically yellow and black. Silver blades are not recommended as they have poor long-distance visibility in this type of water condition.

Spinner Fishing For Muskies In Clear Water (Midwest)

When fishing in clear water, "rainbow trout," "brown trout," silver with white bucktail, and gold with fire tiger tail are popular. In clear water, the best steelhead spinners are:

1. Brown and Black
2. Gold and Green/yellow
3. Silver and Black

When a "rainbow trout" spinner with black spots spins rapidly and is seen from long distance, the blade often looks dark brown. Paired with a bucktail, it is a brown and black lure. The "brown trout" pattern is also a brown and black lure. When the silver lure with white bucktail is viewed through a clear-water filter from the "See Best" System, the red thread and feathers turn black, and the spinner appears "silver and black." The gold with fire tiger bucktail is a muskie version of the gold and green steelhead spinner.

When both musky and the steelhead live in warm clear water, the musky and steelhead spinners look similar. The main difference is that the musky spinners are larger and must provide a wider side view.

The main thing to realize is that bucktail (and thread) tends to be much darker under water than it appears in air, particularly with the orange, red, and purple colors. Late in the summer, some musky fishermen switch to large willow leaf-bladed spinners to reach depths of 10 to 12 feet. Popular colors are a silver blade with a black, purple, or red bucktail. At a depth of 12 feet, all three of these tails will turn black. With all three of these spinners (when fishing deep), fishermen are using a silver and black pattern.

It appears that when spinner fishing for muskies, the colors are the same as for steelhead when you take the underwater appearance of the bucktail or squirrel tail into consideration. Due to the amount of water resistance caused by these bucktails, a #5 musky spinner must weigh between 3/4 of an ounce to 1 1/4 ounce, compared with a #5 steelhead spinner which weighs about 1/2 an ounce.

Optics

It is interesting that fishermen often state that they are "matching the hatch" or matching local forage fish, however patterns of effective lure colors are often explainable in terms of underwater visibility. The local "forage" usually has natural camouflage, thus is not colored for maximum visibility. Lures which may appear to resemble natural food sources while viewed in a stationary position in natural sunlight, may often appear very different under water, yet still remain very effective.

Different patterns of lure colors may be effective for the same species of fish (example: steelhead) in different types of water clarity. Similar patterns of lure color tend to be effective for different species of fish (example: steelhead and muskie), when these fish hold at similar water depths in water of similar clarity. Different patterns of lure colors are effective for the same species of fish, when they hold at different depths of the same water.

I believe that "matching the hatch" may be true from the standpoint of lure size or profile, but that coloration is often more related to underwater optics. There are numerous charts which show the "favorite color" of lure to use on a particular species of fish. Different species of fish hold at different depths in a given body of water. This is what determines the most effective color to use. You can catch rainbow trout, brown trout, and lake trout with the same color lure when all three species occupy the same depth and location in a lake (usually they don't). You will catch spring chinook, fall coho, summer steelhead, and trout with the same lure when all three species are holding at the same depth in the same river.

There are a few exceptions to this rule, such as tournament bass angling or some heavily pressured fly fishing areas, where fish are frequently caught and released. Fish that are hooked repeatedly can quickly become "educated" about the need to avoid striking certain lures. For fish that are caught and released multiple times, there is often value in presenting them with color combinations they haven't seen in the past.

Picture 2-1. A set of drift bobbers, spinners, tubing, and yarn were glued to a bright red plastic board. Here is a photograph of the board taken in full sunlight.

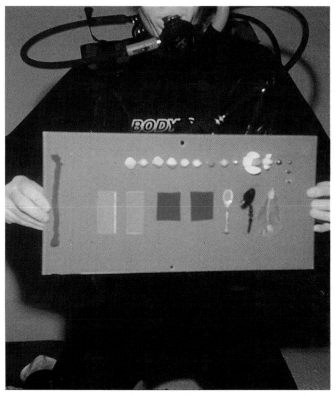

Picture 2-2
The same board was taken into a swimming pool on a cloudy day and photographed at a depth of about two feet. Note that the red plastic board has started to fade at this shallow depth.

Picture 2-3. The diver is sitting at the bottom of the pool, with the board about five feet below the surface of the water. During a cloudy day, note how the board and some of the fishing lures have darkened.

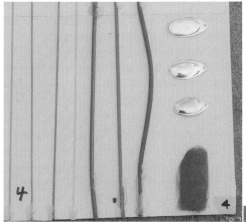

Picture 2-4. Several pieces of spinner tubing, three spinner blades, and some spawn sack were glued to a white plastic board. This is a photograph of the board in full sunlight. Two of the spinner blades are silver, the one on top is nickel plated.

Picture 2-5. The same board was photographed in Washington, at a depth of five feet. This water was green, but considered clear. Please note that one spinner blade fell off prior to this photograph being taken. Two of the red tubing and the red spawn sack are starting to darken.

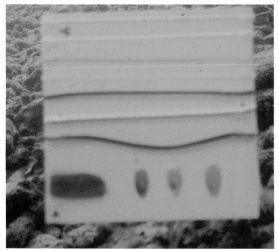

Picture 2-6. The same board was photographed in clear blue water at a depth of fifteen feet. The red tubing and spawn sacks have now turned almost black. Note also that one of the spinner blades has started to darken. The white board appears to be light blue.

Picture 2-7. A set of nine spinner tapes were glued to a white plastic board and a matching set of nine spinner tapes were glued to a black plastic board. Here are the eighteen tapes photographed in sunlight.

Picture 2-8. The board was photographed in green water at a depth of ten feet.

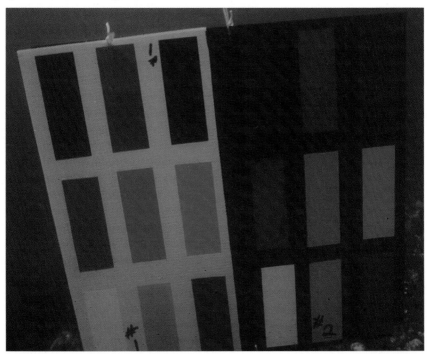

Picture 2-9. The same board was photographed in green water at a depth of forty feet. Some of the colors turned black, while others remained bright. Note that the red tapes which turned black are still visible against the white background, but almost disappear against the dark background.

Picture 2-10. Three marabou jigs, two spinners, a spoon, a drift lure, and plug were glued to a white plastic board and photographed in direct sunlight.

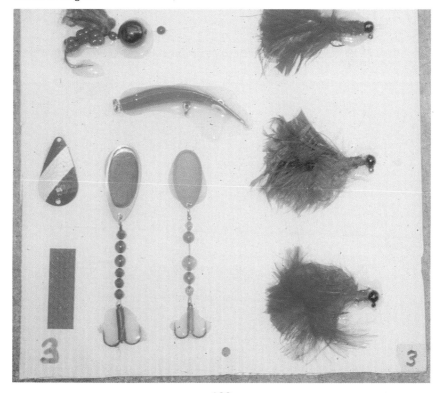

Picture 2-11. The same board was photographed in clear ocean water at a depth of ten feet. Note that six of the lures appear to darken.

Picture 2-12. The same board was photographed at a depth of twenty-five feet. At this depth, six of the lures appear almost black. The white board takes on a light blue appearance.

Picture 2-13. On a sunny day, this board was photographed at a distance of twenty feet. Note how the fish in the picture appear shades of light and dark blue. Also observe how rocks, sand, and other structure appear in the distance. At long distance, on a sunny day, in clear water, dark objects are seen the greatest distance. The color of the white board appears similar to the color of the sand. Against the bright blue background, objects which appear to be dark are very visible.

Picture 2-14. The same board was taken to relatively clear green water in Washington. Even though this was a sunny day, at a depth of forty feet, the background appears almost black. Six of the lures appear black and two of the lures appear extremely bright. The white board appears much brighter than the background. Under these conditions, fishing lures that are the color of fluorescent orange (or white) will have much greater visibility than lures which turn dark under water.

Picture 2-15. An assortment of thirty pieces of spinner tape, blades, spinners, spoons, and plugs were glued to a red plastic board and photographed in direct sunlight. Note that nearly all of these materials appear very bright.

Picture 2-16. The same board was photographed in clear water at a depth of ten feet.

Picture 2-17. The same board was photographed at a depth of twenty-five feet. Observe the darkening on many of the red paints, tapes, and tubing. Also observe the brightening of fluorescent red tape placed against yellow or green. Note that two of the three rainbow trout patterns appear black and white. Only one of the rainbow trout patterns has a pink stripe that shows up. Observe that there is a difference in brightness between the two spinner blades in the lower right corner.

Picture 2-18. The board was photographed at a distance of about twenty feet. Note that the yellow tape in the upper center of the board appears to be very bright. Also note the appearance of the blue tape, compared with the two green tapes.

Picture 2-19. The same board was photographed from the top looking downward. Observe the appearance of the blue tape, compared with the green tapes. Note these colors look different than those in Picture 2-18.

Picture 2-20. Two of the white plastic boards were photographed in deep clear water at long distance. Note that the light fish to the lower left of the two boards is very difficult to see in the light sand, but that fish of the same color stand out against the dark blue background. Picture which of the lures would stand out if placed against the light sand and which would be more visible against a blue background.

Picture 2-21. A similar picture, taken a few seconds later. Note how the fish which were easy to see when they were close, become difficult to see at distance. In this situation, bright fish are easy to see when near and dark fish are easier to see at distance. This is an important set of pictures to study for lure design.

Picture 2-22. This picture is similar to 2-18. Observe the lack of contrast of the red plastic board. Also look at the light and dark colored fish in the lower and upper sections of the picture. See how the black fish blend in with the rocks but show high contrast against the sky. See how the light fish almost appear to disappear when you look up at them.

Picture 2-23. This is a picture taken in shallow green ocean water. Even in very shallow water, many of the items on this board begin to darken.

Picture 9-2. These sixteen items were photographed in room lighting.

143

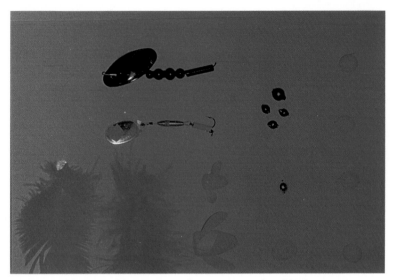

Picture 9-3. In muddy water, only orange and red light penetrates past the first few feet. Under these conditions, many of the colors fade into the background.

Picture 9-4. Four pieces of marabou, dyed deer fur, two red spinners, a spoon, and spinner tape were photographed in room lighting.

Picture 9-5. In deep, green water, only green light is able to penetrate. Note that one pink and one red piece of marabou hold their color, while the other two turn black. One spinner and the reflective tape turns black, while the red/white spoon looks black/white.

Picture 10-1. In deep blue water, only blue light penetrates. This board was photographed with a blue filter.

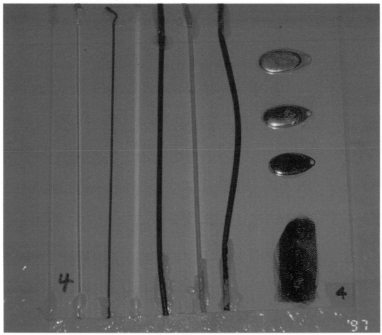

Picture 10-2. This board was photographed with a "See Best" blue filter. See how this picture matches Picture 2-12, which was taken in deep blue water.

Picture 10-3. This board was photographed with a "See Best" blue filter. See how it matches Picture 2-17, which was taken in deep, blue water.

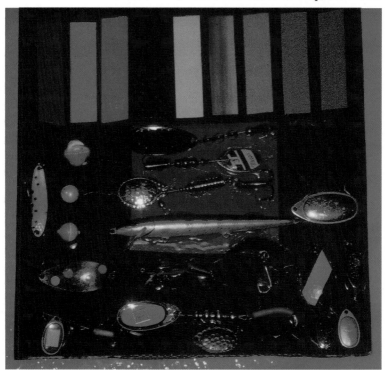

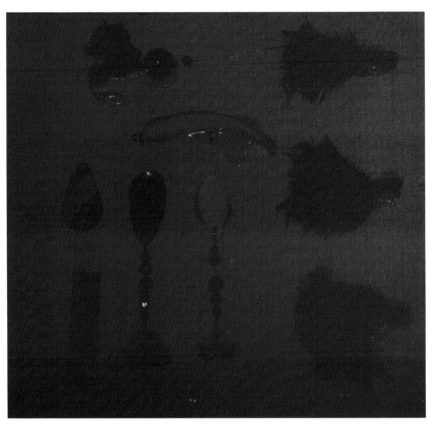

Picture 10-4. This board was photographed with a "See Best" green filter. See how it matches Picture 2-14 that was taken in green water 40 feet deep.

Picture 11-1. Five drift bobbers (metallic red, chartreuse, pink and white, fire red (fluorescent), black) photographed on a light background in room lighting.

Picture 11-2. Simulation of long distance, deep, clear water, and a sunny day (warm water).

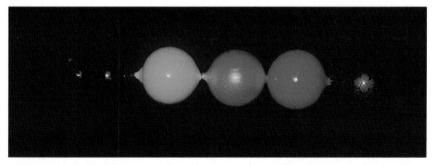

Picture 11-3. Simulation of close distance, deep, clear water, and a dark day. Two of the drift bobbers almost disappear (cold water).

Picture 11-4. Simulation of close distance, deep, clear water, and a bright day. Remember Picture 2-21, bright objects are visible close, but are less visible far away in clear water on a sunny day (cold water).

Picture 11-5. Simulation of long distance, deep, green water, on a bright day. The chartreuse bobber becomes difficult to see (warm water).

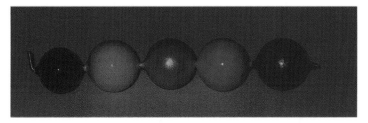

Picture 11-6. Simulation of close distance, deep, green water, on a bright day. The black, non-fluorescent red, and fluorescent red bobbers are the most visible (cold water).

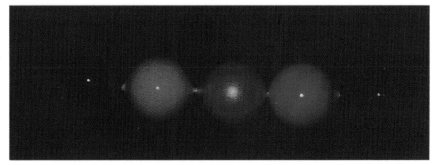

Picture 11-7. Simulation of close distance, deep green water, on a dark day. The fluorescent red and fluorescent chartreuse are the most visible (cold water). This is a common condition for winter steelhead fishing on a cloudy, cold day.

Picture 11-8. Simulation of close distance, deep green water, on a sunny day. Dark bobbers are visible under these conditions.

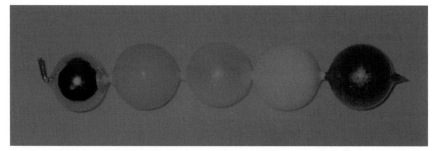

Picture 11-9. Simulation of muddy water on a dark day. Fluorescent chartreuse, pink, and red drift bobbers are visible.

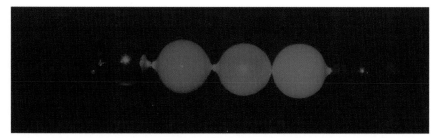

Picture 11-10. Simulation of muddy water on a sunny day. Only the dark bobbers show up. What do you use for fishing muddy water? When testing the same lures in a yellow/brown filter, the combination that shows up best for the two filters and two backgrounds is fluorescent chartreuse and black.

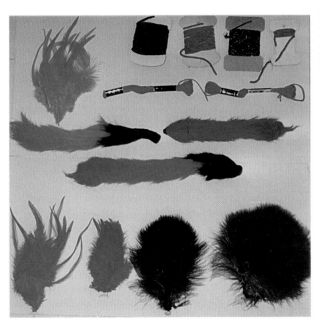

Picture 14-1.
Feathers and fur photographed in room lighting.

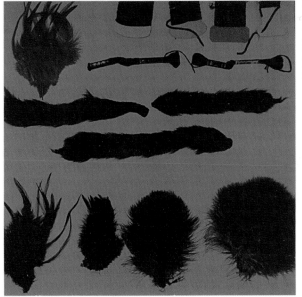

Picture 14-2.
Feathers and fur photographed with a "See Best" green filter. All but one material turns dark.

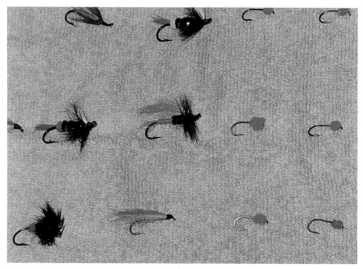

Picture 14-3. When you tie flies, the flies may look bright and colorful in air.

Picture 14-4. The same flies, photographed with a "See Best" green filter. Many of the flies appeared to have three or four colors when photographed in air. In deep, green water, these flies appear to have only one or two colors.

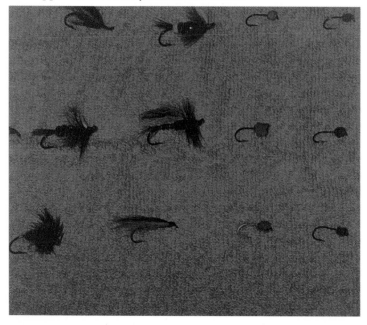

CHAPTER 18

Fishing For Trout, Mackinaw, And Kokanee

SOMETIMES IT SEEMS LIKE EVERY LAKE HAS ITS OWN UNIQUE SET OF "hot colors" that fishermen are using to catch fish. Some lakes have several sets of "hot colors" for different species of fish, that seem to change with the season. Whole books have been written about a single lake. This chapter will examine some of these "hot local colors" and show how they work into the system of underwater visibility.

Fishing For Hatchery Rainbow Trout

Put a worm or Powerbait on a small hook, rig up a sliding sinker, toss your bait into the water, prop it on a forked stick, what could be more simple than fishing for trout on a lake? There can't be much skill involved with it...or is there?

I fished the trout lakes of the San Francisco Bay Area for many years. The urban lakes like Merced, Chabot, Del Valle, and San Pablo receive heavy plants of hatchery fish. Even in these lakes, certain fishermen almost always catch the most fish.

When I first started fishing these lakes in 1986, I averaged about one fish every five hours. Within three years, I got my average up to 14 fish every five hours. I was fishing with the same baits, at largely the same locations, with similar techniques. It was at this time that I came to realize how very small changes can result in major differences in success.

Does the "See Best" System have any relevance to trout fishing in lakes? I admit that I had not developed the "See Best" System in 1986 and did not even consider the importance of underwater color until 1992. It is interesting to examine some specialized trout fishing tactics from the standpoint of underwater visibility. These tactics have proven to be very effective in California lakes like San Pablo, Del Valle, Chabot, Irvine, and Anaheim.

Bait Fishing: If you observe fishermen bait-fishing for trout in lakes, you'll see the most successful technique is usually the sliding sinker with a floating bait, such as an inflated nightcrawler or a prepared bait (like Powerbait). For most shore anglers, it is unlikely that deep-water color shifts play a major role. Many fish are caught within 30 feet of the bank in shallow water. The second most popular bait method is probably bobber fishing with a worm.

When presented below or above the fish, nightcrawlers work better than jar baits. An inflated nightcrawler will often be very productive even when it is suspended only a few inches off the bottom. Trout will rise to take night-crawlers suspended under a float. Prepared baits (like Powerbait, Zekes, Superbait, etc.) tend not to be highly fluorescent under water. Blues, pinks, and reds have limited long-distance visibility in lakes. The best long-distance visibility comes with chartreuse, yellow, glitter, and rainbow combinations. Regardless of the lake or locations, these are almost always the most effective colors. Fluorescent baits have their greatest visibility when suspended well off the bottom.

In general, when using prepared baits, use a longer leader and make sure that the bait floats high. Consider wrapping the prepared bait around a marshmallow or small piece of Styrofoam to get maximum "lift." The most critical factor when fishing urban lakes is where the fish are holding. Often a small change in leader length will make a huge difference in results. There have been weeks where I fished three different urban lakes and found that I needed a 6-inch leader at one lake, an 18-inch leader at another, and a 5-foot leader at a third.

Regardless of leader length, dark baits like nightcrawlers are most effective when presented below or above the fish. Fluorescent baits like Powerbait are most effective when well suspended at mid-heights. My experience was that very thin leaders are more productive when fishing urban lakes. It makes no sense in terms of visibility, since experiments have shown trout have no trouble seeing fine leaders. I suspect that finer leaders allow the baits to sway and move a little more in the current and that this movement may give additional attractiveness to the fish.

The Crappie Jig: A technique that is coming on strong in California urban lakes is the use of a tiny 1/64-ounce rubber crappie jig under a float. In "slightly stained" water, some fluorescent green models have great visibility. On sunny days, the top colors are black/white or pumpkin orange, similar to what you would select for summer steelhead. On cloudy days, the best general-use color is clear or white, which allows the metallic leadhead jig to shine through. This technique uses a long fiberglass trout rod, rigged with a 1-inch bubble, and directly tied to a tiny jig with 2-pound green line.

I feel that the reason these colors are used is that few rubber crappie jigs are made with highly fluorescent materials. I prefer to cast this rig out with a fiberglass rod and slowly retrieve/stop the jig...then "twang" on the line a few times before repeating the process. Some jig experts use a small reel and retrieve the line with a finger extended. In this way, the line slips off the fingers and the jig dances in an irregular fashion.

Lures: In general, silver-plated lures are excessively bright for trout fishing. I stay with the pattern of dark lures on bright sunny days in clear water and painted fluorescent lures in stained deeper water on dark days. The deeper the water the more important the deep-water color shift. The more shallow the presentation, the more important the long-distance color shifts. Lure color selections are quite similar to what is done for similar lighting and water conditions for steelhead—except that silver is seldom used.

Spinner fishing for trout in California closely follows patterns for spinners used in fishing for steelhead in the Pacific Northwest. I found these notations in Ron Kovac's book, *Trout Fishing In California*, concerning the best colors to use in spinners. "Clear days, nickel blades...in dirty water, brass and gold...fluorescent colors are effective on dark conditions...flectolite prism under clear skies...black blades in very clear or very stained water." These are very similar to the recommendations I made in Chapter 12.

Mackinaw

Chartreuse And White In The Great Lakes: In the Great Lakes, there is a considerable amount of suspended organic material in the water. At great depths, it becomes very dark and what little light does reach the depth of 100 feet will be shifted into the yellow range. The brightest colors at that depth are fluorescent chartreuse and white. At depths of 100 to 200 feet, very little light penetrates and the brightest possible lure would be an advantage. When trolling in the Great Lakes with downriggers, chartreuse or "hot white" spoons are very popular. Chartreuse also has the advantage of being the lure color which is visible from the longest distance in this water condition.

Silver, Metallic Blue, And White In Lake Tahoe: In the ultra-clear waters of Lake Tahoe, experts fish for mackinaw with blue and silver plugs and spoons. The lack of suspended organic material allows blue light to penetrate to great depths. The water in this lake transmits up to ten times the light compared with similar depths in the Great Lakes. Because of this increased light intensity, highly reflective surfaces such as metallic blue and silver are very visible. These colors may be visible from up to five times the distance that lures can be seen in Midwest lakes. Metallic blue and silver are the two brightest colors at these depths in Lake Tahoe.

"Brown Trout" And "Rainbow Trout" Patterns In California: For limited periods of time in some high Sierra Lakes, mackinaw may move from depths of 200 feet to relatively shallow areas of 30 feet in early spring. Many anglers claim that they are feeding on hatchery rainbow trout and using these colors will "match the hatch." This statement is not valid because the red stripe on the sides of a rainbow trout turns brown at depths of 30 feet in these lakes and the lure colors do not resemble the color of the trout at these depths. A more reasonable explanation is that the high levels in shallow clear water result in a bright underwater background. Lures which are dark and appear largely black and white give good contrast and visibility. The clear water results in a bright overhead view of the sky and dark patterns like "brown trout" contrast well in these conditions, but would not at depths of 200 feet.

The lesson here is that the same species of fish (mackinaw) will strike three different color patterns of lures when placed in water of different clarity, depth, and underwater brightness.

Silver, Metallic Blue, And White In Crescent Lake: When rainbow trout hold at depths of 100 feet in exceptionally clear lakes like Washington's Crescent Lake, the most effective lure colors match those used for similar conditions to catch mackinaw in Lake Tahoe. The same holds true for many types of deep-water ocean fish in very clear blue conditions.

Brown Trout And Rainbow Trout Patterns For Rainbows In Crescent Lake And Lake Tahoe: When these same fish are holding in shallow water in this same lake, darker colors are effective. Hot local color patterns include nickel/black, rainbow trout, and brown trout. The same color patterns that were effective for catching shallow-holding mackinaw in Lake Tahoe are also the most effective colors for catching shallow-holding rainbow trout in Crescent Lake. In Lake Tahoe these color patterns are equally effective for catching brown trout when they are holding in the shallows with the rainbow trout.

Kokanee: These fish live at a water depth where deep-water color shifts come into play. I know one expert kokanee fisherman who swears by using fluorescent red-tipped spoons when fishing moderate depth, but when he fishes deep he switches to a nickel-plated triple teaser. I know of another expert who uses "laser tape" on his flashers, with the idea that this laser tape will give off multiple colors in deep water.

This was an interesting concept I had never considered. Most non-fluorescent materials would only give off blue light when placed in deep blue water. Nickel- or silver-plated flashers would give off blue light, while non-fluorescent reds and oranges would look black. A fluorescent red would give off red light, but this light would not carry for long distance under water. When you strike a certain holograpic "laser tape" with blue light, it gives off a number of colors—blue, green, yellow, and red. The red gives you short-distance brightness, while the yellows and greens give you greater long-distance visibility. It is important to note that these colors are directional and that it may be helpful to run the tape in several directions, with and against "the grain" in order to increase the likelihood that it will be seen. This tactic would require fairly large flashers to be able to run tape in multiple directions.

Kokanee In Crescent Lake And Lake Tahoe: When kokanee are holding at mid-depths in these clear waters, popular underwater colors are moderately bright like nickel, orange, and chartreuse.

Conclusions Concerning Trout And Landlocked Salmon
The color patterns for effective lure colors appear to be independent of the species of fish. Different species of trout and landlocked salmon will strike the same-colored lure, provided they are holding in water of similar depth, clarity, and underwater brightness. It appears that the reason different species of trout hit different colored lures is because they usually hold at different depths in a given lake.

The testing procedures for identifying effective steelhead lures appear to be valid for numerous species of trout and landlocked salmon in rivers and lakes.

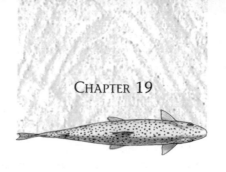

The Eyes Of Other Fish And Lures Used In Bass Fishing

AN IN-DEPTH REVIEW OF THE VISION OF OTHER FISH COULD EASILY double the size of this book. I have decided to hit a few high points of research that may affect the way you use color to fish for other species. Much research has been done on the vision of bass. Extensive research has also been done on non-game fish, such as guppies and cichlids, which may apply to other fish.

An interesting paper, written by Levine and MacNichol, was published in *Scientific American* in 1982. The title of this paper was "Color Vision in Fishes." Many researchers assume that a fish with a primitive body (such as sharks and sturgeon) would also have primitive eyes. Levine and MacNichol disagreed with this statement. They felt that the development of the skeletal system could be independent of the development of the visual system. It is possible that a fish whose skeleton and appearance has remained unchanged for a million years could have a visual system that is quite modern. They state that different species of closely related fish that live in different water conditions can have very different visual systems. On the other hand, unrelated species that occupy the same depth and underwater light conditions tend to show visual systems which are remarkably similar.

The light-sensitive nerve cells in the eye are called rods and cones. Rods contain pigments which are sensitive to low light levels. Cones contain pigments which require more light, but can be used to differentiate color.

Deep-water fish with only one visual pigment in their rods, tend to have a pigment whose sensitivity matches the background light. For fish that live at depths of over 300 feet, the light reaching them is largely dim and blue, with a wavelength of between 470 to 490 nanometers. Shallow marine fish tend to have rods with peak sensitivity of between 500 to 510 nanometers, or blue/green.

Freshwater species of fish tend to have rods which are sensitive to longer wavelengths of light, although not quite so long as the light which actually

reaches them. Rod pigments from fish that live in deep to medium-deep fresh water, tend to visual pigments with maximum sensitivity to 540 nanometers (yellow), even though the light reaching them may tend to be in the orange-red band.

The cones in the eyes of fish tend to be more closely related to the color of the light that reaches them under water. Most saltwater fish that live at intermediate depths lack visual pigments that absorb red light. Their cones are maximally sensitive to blue and green light.

In fresh water, light is red-shifted rather than blue-shifted. The pigments in the cones of freshwater fish are often highly adapted to the light conditions in which they feed. Consider three unrelated types of fish that exhibit similar patterns of feeding and underwater activity—the bluegill, walleye, and piranha. These fish have very few blue-sensitive cells in their eyes, although they do have green and red sensitive cells. They are primarily active near the surface at dawn or dusk and drop down to feed in deeper water at midday. The amount of light reaching them remains fairly constant. Their red-sensitive pigments make them more sensitive to red colors than humans. With walleye, the peak sensitivity to discriminate between different colors lies in the green/yellow range.

Fish that live in deep, brown water tend to have dim light rods and red-sensitive cones. Many species of catfish, bullhead, or the tropical red-tailed black shark will follow this pattern.

The Vision Of Largemouth Bass

What do bass see? It is known that bass have a well-defined color vision system. Bass have traditionally lived in shallow freshwater rivers and lakes and have eyes which are similar in structure to other freshwater fish.

Numerous experiments have been done on bass concerning their vision and ability to identify different colors and thicknesses of fishing line. In one research project, bass were trained to strike targets connected to different-colored fishing line. There were a series of targets connected to colored fishing line, bass were trained to strike certain colored fishing line in order to receive a reward of food. Once the bass learned which color line resulted in a reward, the experiment was repeated with fishing line of smaller diameter.

Bass were able to quickly select the fishing line of the desired color down to four-pound-test line. This experiment was repeated with different-colored fishing line. Bass were also able to discriminate between different colors of the fishing line with a high degree of accuracy. This experiment proved several things. Bass have highly developed color vision and were able to determine the differences between clear, purple, green, blue, yellow, and pink fishing lines. Bass apparently have a fine degree of visual acuity, being able to see very thin fishing lines without difficulty and from a long distance.

Bass are often successfully caught on fishing lines that are 2 to 5 times this heavy. It is safe to say that when a bass strikes a lure, they almost certainly see the line connected to the lure. Apparently bass do not equate fishing line with danger (bass don't think!) and the presence of fishing line coming out of a lure is not a problem.

If bass can see fishing line, why do some fishermen claim ultra-light tackle results in more "hook-ups?" It is likely that this success is more related to reduced line drag, resulting in greater lure action, sensitivity, and control. Studies have shown that thinner-diameter fishing lines result in greater depth and amplitude of movement for fishing jigs, spoons, and plugs. Studies have also shown that reduced line diameter can result in decreased line belly.

Very few studies have taken place which test whether one particular color of fishing line is more productive than another. There was a study where a group of fishermen took turns fishing for bass with lines of a different color and the catch rates were tabulated at the end of the year. In this study, the most productive lines were clear and blue-green. The least productive lines were fluorescent yellow, which caught less than half as many fish. This study was done only with bass and during a clear summertime condition at one lake.

The importance of vision for bass was examined in a series of experiments where bass were made artificially "blind" through the use of opaque eye shields. "Blind" bass in tanks had little difficulty eating, establishing territory, or fighting off other bass. Blind bass were able to locate and eat minnows, crawfish, shrimp, and worms in a matter of seconds after they were dropped into tanks. Researchers noted that the "blind" bass appeared to become more aggressive. These bass were able to identify almost immediately which bass in the tank were larger or smaller than themselves. For these bass, a well-adapted system of smell and sense of vibration appeared to compensate for a lack of vision.

Colors For Bass Lures

Certain types of lures are popular with bass fishermen—plastic worms, crankbaits, spinner baits, "pig and jigs," and small jigs. These differ from the lures used in steelhead fishing in terms of materials and the depth at which they are fished. The colors of these bass lures are also heavily affected by the color of local food sources.

Plastic Worms

More bass are caught on plastic worms than all other artificial lures combined. In some parts of the country, large 7-inch worms are popular, while in other parts of the country, the majority of fish are caught on small 4-inch worms.

Ron Kovac published a chart on worm colors in his book *Bass Fishing In California.*

Clear Water	Stained Water	Muddy Water
Smoke	Chartreuse	Chartreuse
Blue	Black	Black
Pearl	Orange	Orange
Red	Cinnamon	Orange
Purple	Fluorescent fire tails	Fluorescent fire tails
	Bright Day	Early Morning
	Metal flakes	Darker patterns

These suggestion have much in common with the colors recommended for fishing steelhead with marabou jigs. Blue, purple, non-fluorescent red, and dark patterns like smoke (black/white), are effective for fishing summer steelhead in clear water. Metal flakes are not presently used on steelhead jigs (but they could be). As was stated earlier in this book, Mike Laverty recommends using metallic plugs on bright days. Jim Bradbury recommends dark (black) jigs in the early morning, shifting to colors later in the day.

Chartreuse and black are the two most visible non-fluorescent colors in stained and muddy water. Brown is used in all water conditions because it comes close to the natural color of worms. But if added visibility is needed in stained or muddy water, fluorescent fire tails are added to this base color and can be very effective. "Black and white" or "cop car" are considered by many steelhead plug, spinner, and fly fishermen to be their multi-purpose color. A highly effective year-round winner in the plastic worm area is the "salt'n pepper," a clear smoke-colored worm with flakes of black glitter.

Crankbaits

Colors for crankbaits tend to match the colors of forage bait if they are fished in shallow water. In shallow water, color shifts do not take place and baits which match the surface colors of natural food are often most effective. If bass are feeding on frogs, frog patterns would be effective. If they are feeding on shad, silver, glitter, smoke, or clear would be good choices. In many parts of the country, crawdad-colored crankbaits are a good first choice.

In many bass lakes that become stained the most effective crankbaits are chartreuse with a rattle. Several bass articles have stated a "secret" technique of striping a chartreuse plug with an orange marker pen, quoting the author, "For what reason, who knows? But the fish seem to really key in on the added orange stripe." As I see it, the reason is that the orange stripe turns black in deep, stained water, and this gives the added contrast of a dark stripe against a bright chartreuse background. Chrome and blue are effective in clear blue water.

Spinner Baits

Colors on spinner baits closely match suggestions for steelhead fishing spinners and plugs. Nickel blades are best for sunny days, painted fluorescent, chartreuse, or copper blades are best for darker days or stained water. Gold or brass blades are for "in-between."

"Pig and Jig"

"Pig and jig" tends to be a shallow-water technique used in warm water with temperatures over 65 degrees. In clear water, black, brown, and purple are popular. (Purple is only visible in clear water).

In green water, use black or a mix of chartreuse and black. For muddy water use orange/black or black/chartreuse. Both of these non-fluorescent colors will give you a "black/white" contrast in muddy water—a greater contrast than if white were actually used because the light coming through the muddy water will be either chartreuse or orange.

Basic Conclusions About Bass

Bass can see fine detail and colors very well. They are an actively feeding predator that lives in a wide range of depths and water clarity. For shallow techniques like twitchin', jerkin', rippin', poppin', chuggin', and buzzin', lures should match the dominant food source of the area. Effective top-water lures are colored to match shad, crayfish, frogs, or whatever else on which the bass appear to be feeding. Surface color matches are effective, since deep-water color shifts do not affect the appearance of surface or shallow water lures.

Deep-water lures for clear water are effective in silver and blue. Deep-water lures in stained and muddy water appear to closely follow the patterns of non-fluorescent steelhead lures used in similar lighting and water clarity conditions. When fluorescent colors are used, they are usually used as an accent to set off the color of natural bait. This is the second major difference between bass and steelhead lure color patterns. For steelhead, the entire lure is designed for maximum underwater visibility since steelhead are not keying in to natural food sources. For bass, the majority of the lure is a natural color and high visibility accents are placed on the lure to give it greater visibility in stained or muddy conditions. If fluorescent colors are not used, the best way of getting visibility is to design "salt'n pepper" type patterns, taking underwater color shifts into consideration.

It is important not to overestimate the value of color in a bass lure. Since bass hold largely in slow-moving or non-moving water, scent, vibration, noise, and other factors are far more important than they are for fishing steelhead. A blind bass could easily survive in the wild, this has been proven by experiments artificially blinding bass. Bass can hunt, swim, fight, and establish territory without vision.

If all other factors are equal in terms of lure design, movement, scent, and vibration, and the factor of dominant local forage is taken into consideration, bass lure coloration closely follows patterns based on lighting and water clarity. This is an area I expect to be investigating heavily in future years since I am close to signing a contract with a major company that designs bass fishing lures.

Panfish

Bluegills and perch eyes have a great number of light-sensitive nerves for the red/orange colors. Fishing color studies indicate that red/orange flies catch more bluegills than other colors. Jigs with non-fluorescent red thread are very productive when fished near the surface.

Ocean Fish

Different species of fish have different light-sensitive color pigments in their eyes. In deep ocean water, only short wavelength blue light is able to penetrate. Many deep-water fish have an abundance of the pigment chryopsin in their eyes which responds to this type of light. Rhodopsin is a pigment found in the rods of many land animals and in ocean fish. It is a pigment that is sensitive to low illumination blue/green light. It is the dominant visual pigment in salmon and steelhead when they are in the ocean. Porphyropsin is a common visual pigment in freshwater fish like perch and bluegill. It is responsive to longer wavelength light, such as orange and red.

Most of the fish pursued by sport fishermen are advanced fish species with bony skeletons. Primitive fish such as shark and sturgeon have considerably different eye structures. It is thought that the shark may be one fish that lives with absence of color vision. The primitive sturgeon has an eye which uses a system of color filtering oils in the eye to affect the color of light passing through the nerve cells. The presence of color filtering oils would indicate that sturgeon probably don't see certain colors very well, but probably have a fine differentiation of similar-looking colors.

This would make sense when you consider that sturgeon are bottom-dwelling fish and are not exposed to the full range of colors in the visible light spectrum. Deep ocean water would filter out everything except the blue/green, greens, and possibly yellows. The presence of a yellow optical filtering oil would also reduce the amount of blue and red light coming through to the optical nerve cells. The suggestion is that sturgeon should have the ability to differentiate small differences in shades of blue/green.

It is thought that tuna and sharks are color blind. These fish have eyes which appear to be best adapted to seeing dark objects against a bright background. One research study on the skipjack tuna proposed that a skipjack tuna's method of feeding was actually adapted to the type of black/white vision that this fish exhibited. This researcher observed that tuna appear to strike their prey from directly below, possibly because they are able to see the profile against a bright sky.

Concerning vision, color, and other fish I think it reasonable to make certain basic comments. In water which is still, or with fish which are slow moving, other factors such as scent and hearing play an increasingly important role. If fish are feeding on a particular bait source, it is likely that this "live bait" would be a productive lure. Matching the underwater appearance of this "live bait" should also be effective.

In bottom fishing, many fish have eyes which see dark objects against a dark background. On the bottom of the ocean, slow-moving rivers, and lakes, dark lures or baits are visible but scent is probably of much greater importance. In oceans at moderate depth, fluorescent blue-green lures give you the greatest long-distance visibility. If you are fishing in an ocean at eye level, this should be your first choice. In shallow freshwater fishing, many fish will see both fluorescent and non-fluorescent red and orange lures without difficulty. On a sunny day, against a bright surface film, regardless of species, dark browns and blacks will give greater contrast.

If you are fishing a predator and there is a bait source—such as minnows, frogs, insects, shrimp—consider what color the food source may appear to be at the depth of water where the food source is present. A minnow that is silver white, when in blue water 30 feet deep, is likely to appear blue. Fishing with a blue lure may more closely approximate the food source than a lure which is silver or white. Attempt to match the underwater color of the food source rather than the color of the food in air.

If a game fish is actively keying in on a certain baitfish, it is unlikely that fluorescent painted lures will match the underwater appearance, even if they are similar to the appearance in air.

In deep water, white is a fairly universal color since it will alter its appearance to vary with water clarity. When using white lures or baits, it is helpful for the material to be as white as possible. Any tendency to have a yellow or pink tint will result in significantly less brightness at great depths. A "secret" with many fishermen who fish cut herring is to bleach it in a commercial "blue bleach." When viewed from under water this causes the pinkish-white herring to take on a blue-white appearance. The increase in brightness (and effectiveness) of this bait can be surprising.

Color, detail, brightness, location, distance, movement, velocity, and orientation are all factors which can be measured by vision. We've all had the experience of looking for something and not being able to find it. Yet if the object that we are looking for is moving, it becomes very easy to see. Many animals have a greater number of "movement detector" nerves located in the "peripheral vision" portion of their eyeballs. These animals (including man and many fish) are best able to detect movement in objects that they are not looking at directly.

This property can be used or interpreted in two different ways. If all objects under water are stationary, an object which is moving will attract attention. An object needs to go only a slightly different speed than the background in order to be noticed. "Movement" can also be defined as when the current is moving slowly, while the lure is held stationary. If a lure is stationary when dust and underwater debris is moving, it will also attract attention.

"The Beginner's Mistakes"

As fishermen, we have more in common than we have differences. In gathering material for this book, I came upon a chapter written by Ron Kovac in his book *Bass Fishing In California* which he titled "Beginner's Mistakes."

I am going to summarize his comments and ask you to consider their applications to steelheading.

"Wormin': slow down!... novice fishermen are too quick at pulling bait through submerged structure."

"Crankin': put the plug where the fish live... [don't be] overly cautious [about losing your lure to snags in deep cover]."

"Spinnerbait: fish the fall... [slow the retrieve to] drop the lure into pockets behind structure."

"Jiggin': maintain control and feel for the lure... not too tight, not too loose."

"Flippin': hit the target accurately."

And my favorite "Kovac Quote:" "Some people say that the more you fish, the better you get... But if a [fisherman] persists in fishing the same way week after week, it won't matter how much time is spent on the water, as the mistakes repeat themselves."

This is one of the goals of this book, to show that different types of fishing have much in common, and that the concept of underwater optics can have important applications to many types of fishing.

My favorite "Dr. K" quote is: "Practice does not make perfect, practice makes permanent. If you spend a lot of time doing something wrong, you will simply increase the chances that it will happen again."

Information about underwater color, what fish can see, and how lures should be designed can give you a new outlook on what you should be practicing when you fish. Practicing with a purpose gives you a greater chance that you will become more skillful in less time.

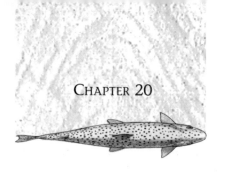

A Day On The Ocean

IT WAS A RAINY NOVEMBER MORNING WHEN OUR SHIP PULLED OUT OF Depoe Bay. Although I grew up on the ocean and had done extensive ocean fishing as a child, it had been almost 20 years since my last time on a boat. As I looked around at the other seven people in our boat, five of them were obviously "veterans," bringing with them a great deal of bait and tackle. Two were apparently "beginners" and knew little about the operation of a fishing reel. I brought no equipment. I looked at the gear present and found myself examining their actions from the aspect of what was actually happening under the water.

I had limited options and had never seen tackle rigged in this fashion. A 40-pound-test monofilament was looped and a large jig was placed directly on this loop without a leader. At the bottom of the line was a large sinker molded around what looked like a 3/0 double hook. What ran through my mind was "Why would a fish hit a bare sinker?"

The jigs were very simple—a large 4/0 hook with red and yellow nylon line, and a red, yellow, or orange body. The jig colors were non-fluorescent and dull, I had no question that all of them would turn dark in the 50 to 70 feet of water that we were planning on fishing. This rig was thrown directly over the edge and dropped to the bottom without adding any bait to the hooks to increase attraction.

The thought that ran through my mind was "Why do they rig like this?" The only conclusion I could reach was that fish were so plentiful in the bay that it was easy to reach a 15-fish limit within a five-hour trip. This rig made it simple for the assistants on the boat.

Unfortunately, this was not a good day. After hitting five different spots and fishing for four hours, five of us had nothing and the entire boat had caught only four fish. The captain sounded frustrated and said that we would return and fish just off the dock. Finally, we began hitting fish. In an hour and a half, we picked up 50 fish. During this period of time, I outfished the other fishermen on the boat combined. Without the benefit of being able to add bait to my line or to change lures, I had only one option.

The captain told us to drop the line to the bottom and jig. As the boat drifted, we were to let out line in order to remain in contact with the bottom. The problem was that people did not "visualize" what was actually happening. Since we were close to the shore, we drifted quickly. Within a minute, the boat drifted far enough that line was dragged out at an angle. At this point, "jigging" probably did not bounce the rig off the bottom. One of two things happened, the rig simply dragged back and forth on the bottom or line belly lifted the rig off the bottom. Result: few bites after the first 10 to 20 seconds (Figures 20-1 and 20-2).

Diagram 20-1
Jigging gets the bait further off the bottom when the boat is above the bait.

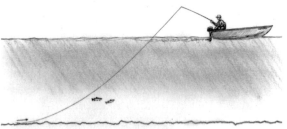

Diagram 20-2
As the boat drifts, jigging fails to get the bait off the bottom.

The only alternative was to go to the end of the boat, throw "upstream" and drop the line to the bottom as the boat drifted over my line, then jig about a dozen times before reeling back up and starting again (Figure 20-3). This is kind of like "drift fishing" except that the boat is moving as opposed to the lure. This allowed my rig to stay in the "strike zone" for much longer than the other fishermen on the boat.

The jig they used was basically black/white. The sinker was lead gray. I had three situations where I caught fish on both the jig and the sinker at the same time. As I have written in earlier chapters, many fish have eyes which allow them to see dark against dark in their lower field. Although I had never before considered the possibility, it makes sense that if a fish is going to hit a sinker, it will be when the sinker is placed below it, rather than at eye level.

Although I couldn't change lure colors, I did have the advantage of being able to think of my lure as it would look to the fish. Visualizing what the lure looked like to the fish made me change my presentation.

Colors For Ocean Fishing

If I were to go back out on this charter, I would construct my own jigs prior to launching. I would keep the jig the same size and make one of them purely black/white and the other with fluorescent red/green yarn. I would put two jigs on line off short droppers and add a piece of green yarn to the bottom sinker. I would then add scent to all three lures. I would alternate the position of the red and black jig.

My thinking is as follows: If the fish were suspended slightly above the bottom, they would drop down and be better able to see the black/white jig or sinker. If the fish were deep and seeing the lure at eye level, they would respond better to the bright green yarn at long distance and the fluorescent red yarn at short distance. Because of the extreme depth that we are fishing, I would not worry about "spooking" a fish by having its appearance shift from gray to red when it moves in. As long as I was hitting some fish on the sinker, I would

Diagram 20-3

Diagram 20-3

By casting "upstream" and allowing the boat to drift, jigging can get the bait off the bottom for a longer period of time.

169

place the lures (from shallow to deep) red/green, black/white, and finally sinker.

Green Water In The Ocean Is Different From Green Water In A River

Most of the suspended material in the ocean consists of fine particles of sand (inorganic). Much of the suspended material in Western streams and rivers consists of decaying plant material (organic). The exception to this is if you have a river which is having water supplied through heavy glacial melt. In most cases, the underwater appearance of green water in a river is green/orange. Ocean water with a similar color (above the surface) would take on a green/gray cast under the water.

In terms of underwater color shifts, this means that ocean water tends to transmit more blue light, and river water more yellows and orange. In freshwater lakes with heavy dissolved organic material, only red light penetrates more than a few feet below the surface.

This difference between light transmission in sea water holds important implications for saltwater anglers. In shallow water, metallic green/blue, and white are very powerful in their ability to be seen at long distance. These lure colors are much more effective in salt water than they are in fresh water. At mid-level depths, fluorescent colors in the blue/green range are very visible and effective. Fluorescent orange is quite visible in deep water but is limited by its inability to be seen at long distance. A white lure is effective in a variety of different ocean conditions.

In the ocean, an angler could do quite well by limiting himself to white, plus metallic and fluorescent colors in blue and green. This is clearly not the case in river fishing. Because of the depth that people ocean fish, it would be wise to avoid non-fluorescent red and orange lures.

When fishing with cut bait, smell is probably the most important fish-attracting element. Some herring skin tends to have a slight pink cast to it. If this pink cast can be removed through the use of a bluing bleach, the result is a "silver-blue" bait that will have significantly greater underwater brightness than the natural "silver-pink," which would tend to turn gray in deep water.

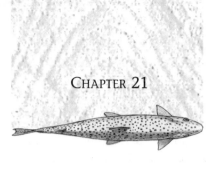

The X Files

"I USE A STAINLESS STEEL SHAFT, A BRASS BLADE, A GOLD-PLATED HOOK, a nickel-plated clevis"... states the angler, "to make the spinner generate an electrical field that fish find very attractive."

ESP And Electromagnetic Fields

"The X-Files" is a popular TV program based on ESP, extra terrestrials, and other non-provable phenomenon. Some fishermen talk about properties of their "secret lures" as having powers beyond the realm of human perception—the fish's ability to measure electrical fields. Researchers have measured the response of sharks to electronic stimuli of .01 volts—equal to a pair of flashlight batteries placed nearly 1000 miles apart! They were able to respond to that level of voltage.

"Ampullae of Lorenzini?"

This skill was based on a structure known as the "lateral line," known to exist in sharks and thought to exist in other fish as well. The electromagnetic sensory structure in a shark is termed the "Ampullae of Lorenzini." In the act of swimming through the water, every fish generates electrical current. Every fishing lure which is built with different types of metals also generates some sort of electrical current as it moves through the water.

We have known about the presence of these electrical nerve receptors since the 1700s but little practical understanding has come from it. A method for measuring these electrical fields has not been developed, nor has there been any research on what type of electrical field a fish might find attractive or unattractive.

When an animal (or fish) moves it generates a small electrical field. When a fishing lure moves, through the water it generates a small electrical field. The size of this electrical field can be increased by increasing the movement and using metals with differing ionic properties. Randomly using as many different types of metal as possible does not automatically increase the electrical field. This latter idea is kind of like saying that people make noise when we move. If we wear different types of metal on each part of our body, we would clank and make a lot more noise when we moved. Would this clanking sound like a popular musical concert and attract hordes of people to gather around us? Unlikely!

What is more likely is that people around us would find this clanking to be an irritation and would avoid us. For sound to attract fish, it has to be something that they naturally hear, not just something loud. I have successfully "called" fish a few times by using a large rock to thump the ground. On the other hand, dropping a tackle box on the bottom of an aluminum boat is an almost sure way to end fishing action.

It is possible that the electrical fields given off by an injured baitfish can call predators to the area. It is also possible to increase electrical fields by pairing certain metals in a spinner. Which electrical fields attract fish and which ones are an irritation? Nobody knows. If an angler catches a fish with this combination, is it the result of electrical field, or simply that the added metal color is more visible? Nobody knows.

Smell

The only ESP research of practical application to fishermen (that I know) concerned the sense of smell and salmon. In these experiments, salmon were directed up a fish ladder in which the current was split by a "Y." Water flow between the two branches were equal and an equal number of fish were observed to take a right or left turn at this "Y." After counting a significant number of fish making these choices, a bear paw was placed in the water flow of one branch. Almost immediately the flow of salmon changed and virtually 100 percent of the salmon shifted away from the branch of the fish ladder where the bear paw was present. The bear paw was removed and placed into the other branch of the fish ladder and the process reversed. Nearly all the fish shifted away from the branch of the fish ladder containing the bear paw.

This experiment was repeated using a human hand with similar, although not as dramatic, results. Through these experiments, a number of chemicals in skin oil were identified which salmon apparently consider offensive. The most dramatic result came from a material known as L-serine. This common amino acid is found in the skin oil of almost all people.

This is perhaps the most often quoted experiment concerning the exceptional sensory abilities of salmon. The concentration of this material that salmon were able to detect was on the order of parts per billion. With this experiment proving that certain smell tracts were unattractive to fish, it brought up the possibility that certain smells may be attractive. It has been estimated that some dogs have the ability to recognize trace materials in the air through smell with over a thousand times the sensitivity of humans. It has been estimated that some fish have a sense of smell that exceeds that of man by over a million times.

I find this information very interesting but the fact remains that tens of thousands of fish are caught each year by fishermen using a drift bobber, spinner, fly, or jig with no scent added.

The Problem With ESP

It is common that fishing authors write about how fish are able to see colors that humans cannot see, hear things that humans cannot hear, and feel electrical impulses that humans cannot feel. Outdoor authors have written about using this to enhance your catch rate. How can something be used to enhance your fishing success when you have no way of measuring it or understanding what about it is attractive? Consider the problems of trying to design a fishing lure to give off attractive electromagnetic fields.

I know of no way of measuring the emission of electrical fields under water. Even if they exist, I know of no way to differentiate between the different types of electromagnetic properties which are attractive or repulsive to fish. I know of no way to measure how water temperature, pH, salinity, and hundreds of other factors affect these fields.

My personal feeling is that a fisherman trying to develop an electrical field to catch fish—without being able to measure this field—is kind of like a blind person who has never had sight trying to paint a picture. I don't doubt that it's possible, but it's not likely. It would be easier for a blind person to paint a picture they would find objectionable, than it would be to paint one that they would love.

I have heard of one guide who claims that he uses an ohm meter in his boat to determine if he is producing attractive electromagnetic fields. I cannot state whether he is doing something useful, but I can say that electromagnetic radiation is very complicated. It is true that an ohm meter measures one aspect of electrical current, just as it is true that a light meter measures one aspect of light. To me, this is like saying that you can go to an art museum with a light meter and determine which paintings people will consider more beautiful. This is very unlikely.

If a top, experienced guide claims to use such a method to catch fish, I would say the real reason he is successful is because he is a top, experienced guide. He probably knows all the best places, best lures, and the best times to fish. I would have a greater inclination to believe this claim if it were made by a less experienced fisherman who was successful in spite of not having this huge background of experience.

People claim to have developed lures colored with dyes humans can't see or that emit sounds we can't hear. I read an article that proposed polar bear fur was better than white calf because it reflected large amounts of ultra-violet light that humans couldn't see. This is unlikely. Dyed polar bear is still effective for catching fish, even though the dyes remove all ultraviolet reflection. Perhaps polar bear fur is more effective because it is brighter in blue light and blue water. It may also be the texture and reflection of the fur which makes it valuable in certain conditions.

I propose the following ideas:

Point #1: Fish have a highly developed sense of smell, which is very important for anglers to consider when fishing in oceans, lakes, and slow-moving rivers.

Point #2: Fish are very sensitive to low frequency vibration. This is difficult to duplicate in fishing lures and is in no way related to the high frequency "rattles" that are put in some fishing lures that claim to emit "low-frequency vibration."

Point #3: Many of the differences between the sensory systems of fish and humans are due to differences caused by the nature of water. Understanding how fish see and hear depends largely on understanding how water modifies light and sound.

Point #4: Whether we are going after salmon, steelhead, trout, halibut, bass, or walleye, the fact remains that we pursue an animal with a brain the size of a pea. It is true that we do not understand its sense of smell, vibration, or ESP, but let's look for simple answers before we try to make them complicated. It is my experience that most fishing "secrets" are quite simple. I urge you to look for simple answers.

Section VII
The Conclusion

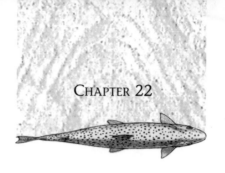

CHAPTER 22

Putting It All Together

THREE MEN SIT AT A TABLE AND DISCUSS FUTURE FISHING LURE DESIGNS for their company. The discussion goes something like this:

"Company X puts out a plug that is green and gold, I think we should too."

"Why don't we put a couple of red stripes on the gills, that would look sharp."

"Maybe we should put a couple of black dots on the top to make it look like a fish."

"Let's do it, hopefully people will buy it."

Lure design and coloration has involved copying popular patterns and making changes based on what the designer considers attractive to humans who see them in air. No thought has been given to what a lure looks like under water. No attempt has been made to custom design a lure for specific fishing and lighting conditions.

The fisherman looks at a rack of pretty lures and picks those that he thinks are attractive. He tries them and hopes that one will be effective. If he catches fish, he buys more and continues to fish it in all conditions. If he fishes frequently with success, he may eventually learn the specific conditions to fish (or avoid) using that lure and color. This process may take years.

Taking It To The Next Level

The information in this book represents a change in attitude. A lure company can build a simulation of water flow, water clarity, and lighting conditions. Based on this simulation, the company would design a lure of maximum effect for a specific fishing condition. The lure company would modify factors related to lure action, color, and weight. The company could then print this information on the label, telling us to use this fishing lure in these specific fishing conditions. Anglers could then purchase lures based on the conditions they expect to encounter. They could benefit from information that would

176

have taken them years of trial and error. Rather than randomly changing lures, in hopes of finding a "hot lure," they stick with a good design and modify their technique. With poorly designed lures, a person might have to make dozens of casts before he is able to place the lure within a few inches of the fish. With a poorly designed lure, you don't know if the fish couldn't see it or just didn't want it.

With a properly designed lure, you know that the fish saw your lure if it comes within a few feet. If the fish doesn't take your lure within the first 3 to 5 casts, then move on, confident that the fish saw your lure every time and was just unprepared to take it. Since you are making fewer casts you begin to concentrate on making each cast better, making each cast count. This reduces your chances of spooking a fish with sloppy technique.

Free of the questions about which lure to use, the angler can cover more water quickly and concentrate on locating fish. He fishes with greater confidence, thus better technique. Having a fishing lure company design a lure based on how it looks and performs *in air* is as crazy as having an aircraft company design a plane based on how it performs *in water*!

What I have done is take accepted solid principles and applied them to another field. This new application of proven concepts represents a major change in attitude. It is my hope that this information will change the way fishing lures are designed.

In 1957, the Mepps spinner came to America. It was a great fishing lure and other companies soon copied it. I was recently visiting the Mepps factory and saw a wall covered with hundreds of Mepps copycats that had gone out of business. There were a few "French-blade" spinners that are still being made.

When any fishing lure becomes popular, numerous people copy it and make changes they think will look good to the shopper. A few of these changes may actually result in a more productive fish-catching lure but this is usually an accident. Usually, lure design is driven by what market research determines will sell. Little or no thought has been given to how a spinner actually looks under the water. Like I suggested before, this is like trying to design an airplane by seeing how it looks and performs under water.

I have read many articles by spinner experts like Jim Bedford and Jed Davis. It is impressive to see the conclusions they reached when their designs were based on the appearance of a spinner in air. Just as many companies have copied Mepps, many fishermen have copied Bedford and Davis, making their own variations. Most of these variations probably don't work because their developers lack the tremendous base of fishing experience of these two men.

What Fish See represents a change in attitude. My understanding of underwater optics explains to me why the Jim Bedford and Jed Davis spinner designs were effective. I look at a spinner (or other fishing lure) based on how it looks and performs under water. Understanding underwater optics allows me to design a spinner in a matter of minutes without having to spend many weeks fishing it before I know the design is effective. No person would consider designing an airplane based on how it behaved under water. Airplane models are designed by putting them in "wind tunnels" or moving-air simulations. Doesn't it make sense to apply the same attitude to fishing lure design?

I design fishing lures by placing them in jets of moving water and evaluating how changes in components affect vibration and movement. I observe spinners under water and through underwater simulations to determine which colored patterns are easiest for fish to see. My research now shows me how the action of a spinner can be altered by changing the style of hook, adding a split ring, or a snap swivel. My research taught me what colors should be placed in which order in which location on a fishing lure. Once one major fishing lure company begins to design lures in this way, I am convinced that others will follow suit.

In 1999 you will see the first spinner that was totally designed on the basis of underwater testing and simulation. I hope that this is the start of a revolution in the fishing tackle industry. I hope to see lures designed using underwater simulations for specific fishing conditions and have this information printed on the package.

I never thought that I would consistently catch 10 steelhead a month. I credit my rapid growth to this change in attitude. Understanding underwater optics has taught me much more than just knowing the best color of lure to use. Understanding what fishing lures look like under water has affected every area of my fishing technique and presentation.

I have learned that this information is valuable for summer steelhead as well as winter steelhead. It works in spring and fall for silver and king salmon. In my investigation for this book I have learned that it explains the effective lures used in different conditions for a wide range of other game fish such as pike, muskie, redfish, trout, walleye, and tuna.

The first level in steelhead fishing is to develop the technique and understanding of what works. The next level is to develop an understanding of why it worked. The third level is to take effective fishing lures, examine them in light of this new understanding and technology, then use this information to design even better products and techniques.

"You Could Make Them Go Broke!"

That's what many fishermen told me during my early seminars. Anglers (steelheaders in particular) are a funny group—strong-willed, independent, competitive—with an "us against them" mentality. They don't trust fishing tackle companies, just like they don't trust used-car salesmen, lawyers, and the IRS. They feel that the lure companies would respond strongly against an accurate system that would allow them to design their lures based on what fish see under water.

As I became more involved in this program, my view of the fishing tackle industry began to change. I believe that many of the companies are now ready for a change in direction. I believe that many tackle companies realize the importance of putting out an improved product.

The color patterns of many popular lures are incorrectly designed but this was not done intentionally. The designers and corporate executives had no idea that the stripes should be running in one direction or another, or that certain colors should not be placed on certain parts of the lure. All they knew was that the lure caught fish and that people were willing to buy it.

A year ago, I ran into an owner of a tackle store that told me he hoped the information in this book would never "catch on," that it could obsolete his inventory. When I first started writing this book a year ago I was thinking in terms of building lures myself, since I felt that existing lure companies would be unwilling to produce lures utilizing this information.

Much has changed since then. On September 1997, I signed a contract to design spinners for Mepps. I will also be designing jigs and soft plastic lures for Mister Twister. I have patents in progress for several spinner color patterns, a new color process for spinners/spoons, and the "See Best" System. This is an exciting time, when fishing lure companies begin to consider what lures look like under water to fish.

I have hundreds of ideas on how to modify crappie jigs, bass worms, spinner baits, minnow plugs, and other lures. But I wonder how far I will carry this since I already have a full-time job in the health care field.

Steelhead Fishing Is About Problem Solving

To me, steelhead fishing is about being outdoors and solving questions regarding the fish. Even though I am still a beginner at this art, there is no substitute for experience. I like to turn this phrase around and be very specific in what I consider "experience." No matter how many years a person has spent on the river, he lacks a major part of this "experience" if he has never gone under water, regardless of how many fish he has caught. I believe that combining the two types of experience will eventually allow some anglers to take steelhead fishing (and other types of fishing) "to the next level."

Why Do Fishermen Know So Little About What Fish See?

Some popular fishing lures are highly visible under water while others are not. This is not the fault of stores or tackle makers. Fishing lure companies and stores are in business for one reason, to provide fishing lures and

179

equipment that the public will buy. There are many items that the fishing public buy because of its advertising. If these items are popular, it would be foolish for a store manager not to include them in his inventory. Very few people understand underwater visibility. If the fishing public is not educated enough to demand high-visibility lures, fishing lure companies will not produce them.

I consider a fish—steelhead, salmon, trout, bass—to be an animal that lives largely by reflex action. They probably don't think a whole lot, and our lack of success in catching them is due more to our misunderstanding of their underwater environment than the high IQ of the fish.

Water filters light. Some light is filtered as it passes through water. Different water filters light in different ways. This filtered light plays tricks on the appearance of our fishing lures. If you understand how water filters light, you can select lures which are minimally affected by certain water conditions. If you use lures that don't change color under water, each fish that you catch will greatly expand your understanding of fishing.

Trial and error is a very ineffective way of fishing when you do not know what you are trying. When you understand what you are actually testing, trial and error can be a very powerful tool. Color has been one of the most misunderstood factors in fishing. For thousands of steelheaders, it remains a point of confusion that can prevent them from ever mastering the sport. Becoming successful in steelheading or other types of fishing does not have to take a lifetime. I urge you not to be concerned with complicated theories or fishing myths. Most fishing questions have simple answers.

Don't Trust What It Looks Like On The Shelf!

The biggest lesson I can teach you is that you cannot trust what a lure looks like on the store shelf. Many lures are labeled improperly and it is difficult to determine what a lure will look like under water. Please closely examine Pictures 14-1 and 14-2. I have put together twelve different fishing materials that were purchased from some of the leading fly fishing and outdoor stores in the Pacific Northwest. All of these materials are labeled "fluorescent." When you look at these materials in air, they all look bright. When you look at them through the green "See Best" filter, some of the materials are five times brighter than others. The term "fluorescent" means almost nothing because it does not state if the material is a bright fluorescent or a dark fluorescent. Fishermen may assume that they are bright fluorescent because they look bright in air. In many cases they are wrong.

My conclusion is this, test your materials and see which give you the greatest contrast in the conditions that you are going to fish. If the water is dark, then use the brightest possible lures. If the water is bright, then use the dark lures. If you do just this, you will not be too far off.

KISS: Keep It Short and Simple

There are four color combinations that I consider most valuable for fishing steelhead or salmon in rivers and streams. I would test the lures using the six major "See Best" System filters. When I say "white" it can also mean silver; "yellow" can also mean brass or gold.

1. Bright fluorescent pink or orange mixed with white, yellow, or green

The best pink or orange will stay bright in five out of six of these test conditions. For winter conditions, this can be your "workhorse"—a combination that some people might use 90% of the time.

Examples: Pink/white Corkie with green yarn or
a silver spinner with pink/green tape/tubing.

2. Black mixed with white, green, yellow, or brown

The black combination will have contrast in all six test conditions. Some spinner, fly, or plug fishermen use this combination as their "workhorse," a great combination during the summer that can be effective in many winter conditions as well.

Examples: Cop car, hot shot, or black spinner with yellow tape/tubing.

3. Green or blue mixed with white or yellow

The best green or blue combinations will stay bright in four of the six test conditions. Some hues of green have poor underwater brightness. In order of effectiveness, I would list fluorescent Kelly green as the best, followed by "lime," "hot prism," and "olive" green. "Forest" green appears to have poor underwater visibility and is of limited use. For clear-water conditions on cloudy days, this combination of green and yellow is outstanding.

Examples: Green Pirate Hot Shot or brass spinner with green tubing.

4. Brightest possible fluorescent red

The best red will stay bright in four of the six test conditions. This is the steelhead fishing version of electroshock therapy! It works best when fish are inactive. Veteran steelheaders use these colors when water is cold and fish are not moving. It also works when fish are holding in deep, almost stationary water. Most active steelhead hold high on a drift, less active ones will be in the tailout. The least active sit at the bottom of deep pools. I have seen this color work very well on summer steelhead that sit at the bottom of 15-foot-deep ponds and appear to be stationary for days at a time, in the middle of summer with water temperatures in the high 60s.

Examples: Red Flatfish or fluorescent red cured roe.

These are the most valuable color combinations for the steelheader. Different sizes and variations of these four color combinations will cover all your steelhead needs. In terms of color, it is very important to find the best fluorescent green hue, the best fluorescent pink, and the best white (including silverplate). If you are a fly fisherman, you must live with the fact that you have many poor colors, depending on numerous different shades of white to build contrast and the illusion of depth.

The color closest to the hook should be the color that is brightest from short distance. The areas of the lure furthest from the hook (or the profile of the lure) should be those colors which are visible from the greatest distance. If you pick lures with the greatest contrast in the greatest number of underwater conditions, you will have lures which are very effective in a range of conditions. If you have a lure which gives off good vibration, movement, or has attractive scent, making it the correct color will only serve to make it more effective.

Final Note

"Best steelheading success often comes to the anglers who learn all they can about the species, its habitat, and life cycle." Milt Keizer, *Western Steelhead Fishing Guide.*

When fishing fast-moving water of limited visibility, understanding underwater color shifts, the physiology of steelhead eyes, and underwater backgrounds, becomes valuable to the fisherman. Do not think of this information as a substitute for experience and technique. Think of this information as something you can add to the skills that you have already developed.

With the proper equipment, understanding underwater visibility can become a powerful tool. The knowledge contained in this book is something that few people understand and even fewer can use. I hope that the information that I have presented to you concerning the fish, their underwater habitat, and how their vision changes during different times in their life cycle, will increase your fishing enjoyment as you learn *What Fish See.*

Thank you for your time and thank you for reading this book. I hope to see you on the river!

Colin Kageyama, O.D., F.C.O.V.D. ("Dr. K")

September 9, 1997

HELPFUL BOOKS AND MATERIALS

"See Best" System
Dr. K   1-800-361-3668
"See Best" System #1, #2, and #3 for testing underwater visibility of fishing lures. Articles, tapes, and seminars.

"See Best" Spinners
Mepps/Sheldons   1-800-237-9877
"See Best" Spinner, redesigned color combinations for the Aglia, Syclops, XD, Thunderbug, and Mepps Fishing Guide.

B.C. Angling Post
Bill Williamson   1-503-655-4161
Bob Toman Trolling Spinners for salmon.

Oregon Fishing Club
Bruce Harpole   1-541-967-8301
River access, private lakes, fishing classes in northern Oregon.

Frank Amato Publications   1-503-653-8108
Color Guide To Steelhead Drift Fishing, By Bill Herzog
Spinner Fishing For Steelhead, Salmon, and Trout, by Jed Davis
Plug Fishing For Steelhead, by Mike Laverty

Marketscope Books
Bass Fishing In California, by Ron Kovac   1-408-688-7535
Trout Fishing In California, by Ron Kovac

Scientific American
"The Mind's Eye," Introduction by Jeremy Wolfe
W.H. Freeman and Company
41 Madison Ave.
New York, NY 10010

Vision Perception, by Tom Cornsweet
Academic Press
111 Fifth Ave.
New York, NY 10003

KOKANEE: A COMPLETE FISHING GUIDE
Dave Biser

Kokanee salmon are found throughout North America. These chunky, tasty lake-dwelling salmon are challenging to catch unless you know the special techniques. Biser reveals all the techniques and various sorts of terminal tackle, baits, and lures. This is the first in-depth book about this wonderful national game fish, the freshwater version of the famous sockeye salmon of West Coast fame. 5 1/2 x 8 1/2 inches, 180 pages.
SB: $14.95 ISBN: 1-57188-120-4

THE TROLLER'S HANDBOOK
Ray Rychnovsky

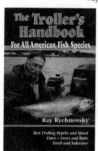

An in-depth treatment of fresh and saltwater trolling methods for all game fish. The author explains how to achieve the most effective trolling speeds and the proper tackle, lines, and gear to use. Dozens of photographs and graphs. Trolling is one of the most practiced but least understood angling techniques. This book will help make you a highliner. 5 1/2 x 8 1/2 inches, 92 pages.
SB: $12.95 ISBN 1-57188-122-0

STEELHEADER'S REFERENCE GUIDE
Steelhead Catch Information Statistics for Determining Where and When to Catch Oregon and Washington Steelhead
Eldon Ladd

This thoroughly researched report/book has complete steelhead catch statistics for Oregon and Washington streams and rivers documented by month.

Hundreds of waters are included, as well as Columbia River dam counts on a monthly basis back to 1938. By using it you can guarantee that you are fishing the right river at the right time for either winter- or summer-run steelhead! Smolt releases for all streams are also included as well for the last 10 years. The information in this report is invaluable for understanding steelhead runs and where the best fishing occurs year after year. 100 pages, 8 1/2 x 11 inches.
SPIRAL: $19.95   ISBN:1-57188-173-5

SPOON FISHING FOR STEELHEAD
Bill Herzog

One of the most effective ways to hook steelhead (as well as salmon) is with a spoon. Bill Herzog covers spoon fishing techniques for the full year, going into finishes, sizes, weights, shapes, water temperature differences, winter and summer fish differences, commercial and custom spoons, spoon parts suppliers, and reading water. Scores of color photos printed on thick, glossy, quality paper enhance the learning experience along with many line drawings, graphs and illustrations. If you like to fish for steelhead and salmon you will find the information in this book to be invaluable—regardless of how you fish. This is a very revealing, post-graduate fishing technique book sure to please! 8 1/2 x 11 inches, 64 pages.
SB: $14.95   ISBN: 1-878175-30-0

SPINNER FISHING FOR STEELHEAD, SALMON AND TROUT
Jed Davis

The "bible" for spinner fishing and the most in-depth, non-fly-fishing book ever written about steelhead and their habits. Information on how to make spinners is complete, including how to assemble, obtain parts, even how to silver plate. The fishing techniques, lure, line color and size selection, and reading fish-holding water sections are excellent. 8 1/2 x 11 inches, 97 pages.
SB: $19.95   ISBN: 0-936608-40-4
HB: $24.95   ISBN: 0-936608-41-2

COLOR GUIDE TO STEELHEAD DRIFT FISHING
Bill Herzog

Each year nearly 1,000,000 steelhead are hooked in North America and the great majority of these fish are hooked using drift fishing techniques. This lavishly illustrated, all-color guide is the "bible" if you want to get in on the action. Written by one of America's greatest drift fishermen, you will learn the techniques that can guarantee your entry into the 10% of the anglers who hook 90% of the steelhead. This is a heavy-duty graduate course! 8 1/2 x 11 inches, 80 pages.
SB: $16.95   ISBN: 1-878175-59-9

IF NOT AVAILABLE IN YOUR AREA ORDER FROM:
FRANK AMATO PUBLICATIONS, INC.
P.O. Box 82112 • Portland, Oregon • 97282 • (800) 541-9498 • FAX (503) 653-2766
Business Hours: 9 a.m.-5 p.m. • Monday-Friday (Pacific Time)
E-mail: fap@teleport.com   Web: www.amatobooks.com